Derek and Nigel
Two Heads, One Tale

Derek and Nigel
Two Heads, One Tale

DEREK BEVAN
NIGEL OWENS

WITH ALUN GIBBARD

First impression: 2018

© Copyright Derek Bevan, Alun Gibbard, Nigel Owens
and Y Lolfa Cyf., 2018

The publishers wish to acknowledge the support of
Cyngor Llyfrau Cymru

Cover photograph of Nigel Owens: Getty Images
Cover design: Y Lolfa

ISBN: 978 1 78461 297 9

Published and printed in Wales
on paper from well-maintained forests by
Y Lolfa Cyf., Talybont, Ceredigion SY24 5HE
website www.ylolfa.com
e-mail ylolfa@ylolfa.com
tel 01970 832 304
fax 832 782

Contents

Introduction

This is a book that nearly didn't happen. Not because of any contractual wrangling with the publishers, nor because Nigel Owens is a globetrotting referee difficult to pin down in one place long enough for a chat. No. But because we nearly lost both men this book is about in a horrific car accident in January 2014.

Four match officials were travelling back from a Heineken Cup game held in the South of France: Sean Brickell, John Mason, Derek Bevan and Nigel Owens. They were on the M4, having dropped Sean Brickell off at the Welsh Rugby Union's National Centre of Excellence, where he had left his car for their trip to referee the Castres versus Leinster fixture. Heading west near the junction for Pyle and Porthcawl, suddenly, out of nowhere, the heavens threw down a torrential hailstorm. The skies went pitch-black, visibility was down to near nothing, the M4 was not safe to drive on – but not possible to drive off either. Nigel, at the wheel, tried his best to control the car, but he was fighting a losing battle. They shot across all three lanes, up the bank and hit the concrete steps – having demolished the steel barriers – where they spun around and landed back sideways across the middle lane of the motorway. The best of German engineering had been concertinaed as if it was an empty tin of beans. That said, all three say that if it had been pretty much any other car, they all could well have been critically injured or killed.

Miraculously, the three passengers walked away from the wreckage severely shocked but with only cuts and bruises. A lorry driver had pulled his vehicle across the lanes, preventing oncoming traffic from ploughing into their car, and possibly fatally injuring them. As they stood there, shaken, at the side of the M4, other cars slowed down to see the damage. Some recognised the casualties. 'Hey, look, it's Nigel Owens!' – an indication in itself that fans, by then, recognised referees. Well, this one at least. On seeing the accident, a few police officers stopped on their way back from work to see if they were OK. Then some other cars stopped as well. Having seen who was involved in the accident, they immediately asked, 'You OK, Nigel?' 'Are you alright, Nige?'

Derek Bevan stood there smiling wryly, and in his usual witty manner said, 'Hey, there were another two of us in the car you know! And yes, John Mason and I are OK, thanks for bloody asking!'

The story hit the headlines the day after, including in *The Times*, again only mentioning Nigel's presence in the accident. Nigel Owens' lucky escape was the gist of all the headlines.

But fate had intervened and two Welshmen, who had reached the top of the refereeing ladder, lived to tell the tale. And this is their tale. In their M4 trauma there is a snapshot of the bigger picture. Nigel gets the headlines, but Derek was there all along. You'll see that clearly on the following pages.

Over the years, quite a few Welshmen have been called the best rugby referee in the world. Clive Norling and Gwynne Walters, for example. Derek has and Nigel is. But only two

Nigel and Derek sharing a joke before the Gowerton v Crymych game – a match Nigel refereed a week after taking charge of the 2015 Rugby World Cup final

Welshmen have refereed the Rugby World Cup final. It's these two. Between them they cover all but one of the World Cup competitions held since the very first in 1987. The only one which didn't involve either of these two is the 2003 World Cup when England were crowned champions. That's a fact that they both smile at with some irony!

That's seven World Cup finals that have had either Derek Bevan or Nigel Owens playing their part in keeping order on the pitch as either a referee or an assistant referee. Only seven men have ever refereed the eight World Cup finals that have been held. Two of them are Welsh and here's their story.

But that's not the only link between them. They have worked together from the start of Nigel's career. Derek has played a major role in mentoring the man now described as the best rugby referee in the world. Since hanging up his whistle, Derek has played an active role as a TMO (Television Match Official) and, of the hundred or so European games refereed by Nigel, Derek has been TMO for over three-quarters of them, as well as being TMO for many domestic league matches.

Suffice it to say that they know each other really well. Add to that the fact that Derek and Nigel are two of the wittiest and funniest men in rugby, and you have the makings of a good book full of rugby stories from the two men in the middle. And here it is. It's Derek and Nigel sharing their experiences of World Cups, global travel, village rugby, awkward players and so much more.

In telling their stories we also get two rare insights. One, of the game of rugby from the referee's perspective. We're more than familiar with the players' view of the game today. But how do the officials see this growing world game? How do they prepare for their matches and who refs the refs?

Also, because Derek and Nigel, between them, span nearly four decades of Welsh rugby, we can see how the game has changed over that long period.

The two men have a huge mutual respect for each other. They are completely comfortable in each other's company. Gathering the material for this book was, firstly, all about finding sufficient gaps in Nigel's schedule for the three of us to meet, but once we did there was no stopping the two of them. Conversation flowed. What we have between these two covers is the personal story of Derek Bevan and Nigel Owens as they have come into contact with each other. They were both open and warm. They were both funny. They both share so much experience of the rugby world, giving us an insight we've not had before.

Derek has been called the Nigel Owens of his day. Or perhaps maybe it's a case of Nigel Owens being today's Derek Bevan. Or maybe Derek is Derek and Nigel is Nigel. Whichever description sits most comfortably, there's no denying that these are the top two Welsh rugby referees ever. So sit back and enjoy the rugby worlds of Derek and Nigel, as it's hello from him and hello from him, with me caught somewhere, sometimes, in the middle!

Alun Gibbard

1

The Tale of Two World Cup Finals

1991 and 2015. Twenty-four years is a long time in rugby. The game Nigel Owens refereed in the most recent final, between New Zealand and Australia, was so different to the one Derek Bevan refereed in the 1991 final between England and Australia. Not so much the matches themselves, although it must be said that Nigel had the better of the two matches without doubt, but more so the structure of the game itself and the way both World Cup finals were prepared for and organised. So, as both referees tell their tale, we also get to see the way the game has changed in the days between Derek's final and Nigel's.

Both finals were played at Twickenham, with England host nation on both occasions, along with Wales, Scotland, France and Ireland in 1991, the first Northern Hemisphere final. But the main difference wasn't one of geography at all. The first final was in the so-called amateur era and the other was very much a professional era tournament. One would have supplied Welsh players from clubs across south Wales, the other supplied the Welsh team with players from only four Welsh regions, and a few players from clubs which played on the other side of Offa's Dyke and across the English Channel as well.

To start at the beginning. How does the referee for that 1991 final, on 2 November 1991, remember that competition?

Derek Bevan To start with, the way referees were chosen for the competition was completely different to the way it happened for Nigel. At that time, each rugby nation was allowed to pick three referees deemed to be the best in their country. The referees' committee of the Welsh Rugby Union – it had to be by committee in Wales didn't it! – would decide who the best three were in Wales. The chair of that committee at the time was Rod Morgan, the Chief Constable of South Wales Police. As the year of the first ever World Cup drew nearer, the top three referees in Wales were myself, Winston Jones and Clive Norling. But only two of the top three would be selected to represent Wales in the World Cup. Winston was the man who missed out that year, with Clive and myself being chosen. That was really tough on Winston I must say. So, in 1987, there were two Scottish referees, two Irish, two French, two Australian and two New Zealanders. That was the team of referees for the inaugural World Cup.

Nigel Owens That's so different to the way it's been done since I've been involved in the same tournament. The referees for the World Cup are chosen according to their performances which, in turn, determine their rankings, and the choosing is done by World Rugby, or the IRB as it was called until 2014. There's a definite structure for evaluating referees and that evaluation determines our world rankings which, in turn, determines if we're chosen for the World Cup or not. The decision about who gets the World Cup final is based on performance during the World Cup itself. You could be going into the World Cup as the world's leading referee, but if you don't perform well in the competition itself, then you won't get the final. It's as simple as that. The only other way you won't get the final is if your home country is playing in it. Then you have no hope, however good you are.

DB You mean you're chosen more on your merit and ability as opposed to us chosen by committee?!

NO No, I didn't say that! The way they assess the merit is different today, that's all. You were all chosen on the basis of how good you were. But today, with far more games than in your day, we are assessed match by match and have a ranking system based on that. It's really strict.

DB That's true enough what you say about the number of matches. I could go 18 months without refereeing an international, whereas you have so many every year, year in, year out. So, in 1987, pretty much every country was guaranteed to have a ref at the World Cup finals. That's far from the case now, as the refs aren't chosen by country.

NO Scotland is a good example of that. They haven't had a ref at the World Cup finals since 1999, when Jim Fleming was there. They have had touch judges and TMOs, but not refs. Today, you might be the best ref in Scotland, but not in the top ten or twelve in the world.

DB Then, as the tournament progressed, there had to be a filtering process to decide which refs stayed on as teams progressed from the group stages to the knockout stages and the number of teams in the competition decreased. Many refs were sent home after the pool stages, and you didn't know in advance how long you'd be at the tournament.

NO That's so different to today! We're all out there for the duration of the tournament. The only difference, moving from the pool stages to the knockout stages, now is that all the assistant referees are sent home and the twelve referees take over the duties of running touch. The four TMOs stay on. So how were you told which referees stayed and who was to be sent home before the knockout stages then? I presume it must have been quite a stringent process.

DB Let me tell you how it happened and you can see how stringent it was back then. It was amazing! We were at our hotel in Auckland, sat around a table, ready for an evening meal: Fred Howard and Roger Quittenton, the two English referees, and Clive Norling and myself. After a while the hotel tannoy was heard, 'Mr Fred Howard, can you come to reception please? Mr Fred Howard.' Fred put his cutlery down and went to reception. He came back looking rather pale. I asked him what the matter was. He said that there was a phone call for him at reception from John Kendall-Carpenter, the chairman of the committee organising the World Cup. We were all anxious to know what the message was. Fred started to tell us. 'I'm going up to Brisbane,' he said, 'to run touch for Wales against New Zealand.'

NO He was told he was staying on, and what game he had, in that phone call?

DB That's right. The three of us then wondered if he knew what the rest of us were doing. He continued. 'Bev,' he said, 'you are going to Sydney to run touch for France against Australia...'

NO What! He actually was given the message over the phone to pass on to the rest of you, as well? No way! Did you expect to be in the semis at all? Was it a case for you of just being glad to be in the finals in any capacity, as it was for me in 2007?

DB It probably was a case of that. I did have ambitions of course, but realised that Clive was probably regarded as the number one in Wales then. But the story gets more intriguing. Clive and Roger were really anxious by then, and wanted to know their fate of course. Fred was questioned further. This time the questions were greeted with a deathly hush, before Fred eventually said, 'You two are on the flight home next Tuesday.' Roger Quittenton didn't believe him and was convinced that Fred was pulling his leg. But he soon realised he wasn't. The night just died. No one finished their meal.

NO I can't believe that two of the top refs in the world were given a message over the phone by a third party that their World Cup was over! Unbelievable!

DB Aye, and over dinner at a hotel too! I felt really awkward. Inside, I was chuffed to have a semi-final at the World Cup, as that was against expectations as far as the pecking order in Wales was concerned. But, of course, I felt really sorry for the two who had to go home, and felt awkward that one of them was Clive. The way they were told was wrong, no doubt about that.

NO Quittenton, of course, was the ref in charge of the Wales All Blacks game when Andy Haden dived out of a line-out, but no penalty was given to Wales. So he wasn't a favourite with the Welsh anyway, was he? Wasn't there a famous story about an incident between Roger Quittenton and you involving some muesli? Was that at the 1987 World Cup?

DB Yes, indeed. Regardless of that decision against Wales, he wasn't an easy man to get on with anyway. When we arrived out there, I was a little late for the first breakfast in Auckland. I walked over to where the Welsh and English refs were at a table having breakfast together and glanced at what each one was having. Roger had a full bowl of fresh-looking muesli. It looked really good and I decided I wanted some. I searched everywhere at the breakfast counter but couldn't find any. I went back and asked Roger where he got it from. 'It's my own concoction; I get it made up for me at home,' he said. 'It's very healthy and helps my concentration in matches. I've measured the portions out to last me the tournament, so I'm sorry I can't give you any.' So, at that table in Auckland, when we had our last supper and Roger was mortified that he was being sent home, so much so in fact that he started to cry, he turned to me and said, 'Derek, haven't you got anything to say?' I was, unusually, a little lost for words for a while before saying, 'Do you know that muesli you had…' He looked at me in total disbelief!

NO That's brilliant!

DB It's fair to say that Roger wasn't well liked by the Welsh, but he made things even worse following a match between Richmond and South Wales Police. He sent a South Wales Police player off and they deemed that he had blown the whole game out of their hands. In the bar after the match, enjoying a drink or two with the Richmond committee,

South Wales Police did not want to spend much time with him because of the way he refereed the game. But he was overheard saying to one of the Richmond men, 'Oh yes, when you referee the Welsh you have to treat them like animals.'

NO No way!

DB Yes he did. But, unfortunately for him and the Richmond committee who chuckled enthusiastically at his remark, it was heard by a reporter from the *South Wales Evening Post*. The headline was obvious: 'Quittenton calls the Welsh animals.' Two days later, my phone rings. 'Derek. Q here.' He called himself Q all the time. 'Bit of publicity going around Wales that's not good for me, I gather.' 'Yes Roger, you're right.' 'I'm looking for a friend in Wales right now.' 'Rog, you've rung the wrong f***ing number!' And I hung up on him!

NO So, back to the World Cup in 1987, Clive and Roger left and Fred Howard and you stayed. So you then had a World Cup semi-final under your belt as an assistant referee. I'm sure you were more than happy with that and more than happy to stay out there longer than you expected.

DB Oh, of course I was! What about your first World Cup then Nige, how did that happen?

Derek at his first rugby World Cup finals in 1987, with Kerry Fitzgerald (Australia), Jim Fleming (Scotland) and Brian Anderson (Scotland)

NO Mine was a full 20 years after yours, Bev! I'd had my first taste of international rugby in 2003, when I refereed a Portugal versus Georgia match. But it was in May 2005 that I had my first taste of a Tier 1 international, when I refereed Scotland against the Barbarians. It went OK, but it wasn't a good time for me as I'm sure we'll talk about later. It was followed by a match in Osaka between Japan and Ireland. I was on the international ladder, at least. But I had to suffer quite a setback that same year. I wasn't chosen as one of the 16 refs who would be in charge of the 16 Autumn

Internationals that year, because I had the lowest score of all IRB refs based on those two games. It took a while and a lot of soul-searching for me to pick myself up from there, but gradually I did. In October 2006 I was chosen to referee my first big European club game, Leicester against Munster. I then had an Autumn International fixture that year, followed by my first Six Nations game, England versus Italy, in 2007. So I had managed to climb up the ladder. All that was left now was for the IRB to recognise that and choose me for that year's World Cup.

DB Wasn't there a match in New Zealand before that, Nige? That was a milestone for you I would say.

NO Yes, there was. My first ever visit to New Zealand. I was chosen to referee Australia against the All Blacks, the Bledisloe Cup. Up until that point I had only been in charge of seven internationals and the media in those two countries made sure that they told everyone how inexperienced I was! But the game went well and it was my performance in that game that got me selected for the World Cup in France in 2007.

DB No doubt you were given a hard time at the pre-match meetings with representatives of both teams as well. They can be quite hostile.

NO I've rarely seen any meeting like the one before that game. I had five of the All Blacks camp in the room with me, including Graham Henry, Steve Hansen and Richie McCaw. They seemed to be quite concerned that I'd be influenced by the fact that McCaw, allegedly, had a tendency to kill the ball on the floor rather too often. The meeting with their opponents that day wasn't less hostile either. The Australian coach was worried that I would be influenced by press coverage about the weakness of the Australian scrum. I just emphasised my complete neutrality; I was not influenced by stories, gossip or opinions. As it turned out, that kind of pre-match referee briefing was banned for the 2007 World Cup and for the next two years as well.

DB And when it came back, it was only one coach per team that was allowed at such meetings. That's a fairer way to do it I would say. Fancy having five All Blacks in the room, including the one they wanted you to be concerned about!

NO When the World Cup came around, I was happy that I had made my way back up to the top 16 referees in the world. I'd only reached the top level of refereeing in 2005. That's when I was officially capped as a Test match referee by the WRU, having worked my way up the ranks. I was then able to referee first-class games, not just the district ones. So I had no thoughts about reffing in the next World Cup after that, in 2007. I knew I just had to concentrate on my game and develop myself as a ref which is what I had done the best I could up until then. Being in the top 16 was more than I could hope for, especially after some difficult times.

Only twelve refs would be chosen for the World Cup. I didn't honestly think that I would make the cut and wasn't at all convinced that I would even be a touch judge. The first nine refs were almost an instant choice, which meant that the remaining three would have to come from the five or six outside the top nine. Technically then, I was in with a shout, but the best I could say was that I had worked my way up to being an outside chance.

But, one day, the phone rang to tell me that I was in the refs' team for the World Cup. What a surprise! To put that into perspective, on a personal level, it was probably more of a surprise when I was chosen for that World Cup than it was to be given the final in 2015. I really was shocked.

DB Who else went from Wales?

NO No one. I was the only Welshman there as a referee. Hugh Watkins was there as a touch judge, so it was good to have a fellow Welshman out there with me.

DB You kept the tradition going then Nige, with the Welsh having an official at every World Cup since the first! But there's a big difference between the four World Cups I was in and the three you've been in so far.

NO What's that then, Bev?

DB There were other Welshmen refereeing in all four of mine but you were the only Welshman in all three of yours. Clive Norling was there in 1987, Les Peard in 1991, Clayton Thomas was there in 1995 and he was in the tournament when it was held here in Wales in 1999.

NO The closest I got was having three touch judges in my three tournaments. Hugh Watkins was there in 2007, Tim Hayes in 2011, and then Leighton Hodges in 2015. So you're right, no fellow referees at all, and the touch judges left after the group stages anyway. It's interesting to note though that there was more than one referee from Wales for the first four World Cups and then only one for the next three.

DB What games did you referee in that tournament then?

NO I didn't look too much into what games I had to be honest, because I didn't mind if I didn't have any of the big pool matches. I was just glad to go and was happy to take whatever I was given and, in that sense, there was no real pressure on me to perform compared to a few of the others who would be vying for the big knockout games and the final itself, of course. I didn't get any of the so-called really big games. I reffed Georgia versus Argentina, Scotland Romania and I suppose the one you could call the biggest,

Fiji against Australia. They all went well, thankfully, which put me in a good position moving forward. I was then given two fixtures in the following Six Nations, in 2008.

DB I suppose that did mean that you were in the mix for the knockout stages though, having had a good run in the group stages.

NO Technically, yes I was. I'd started to think that myself then as well, having had the taste for it. A meeting was called by refs' manager Paddy O'Brien, and the officials for the remainder of the tournament were announced. The names were read out in front of us all. Alain Rolland had Australia England; Argentina Scotland was given to Joël Jutge; Alan Lewis was given South Africa Fiji. Wayne Barnes was given the big one, the host nation France against the All Blacks. The whole room went quiet when that was announced as it was a bit of a shock. Wayne was a relatively new ref and no one expected him to get that one. My reaction to that was thinking that that was a boost for me, in the sense that if he could get chosen for such a big game, as inexperienced as he was, then that could inspire me.

DB That's interesting, Nige. Because I know, and you do as well as I do, that a positive attitude like that isn't always obvious among referees.

NO It's true to say, unfortunately, that there are many refs, not so much on the international scene maybe, but there are refs who delight in the fact that one of their rivals gets a bad game and hopes to be able to move ahead because of another ref's bad performance. I would far prefer to see a ref doing really well, so that then makes me determined to improve my performance to be better than his. That certainly was the case in my first World Cup in 2007, with that Barnes appointment. I wasn't jealous of him at all. When I was in that room, after the announcement, my mind was turning round and round. Well, if Wayne Barnes got that one, I could well have been close myself. Maybe I actually was in with a shout for some of the knockout games. I just knew that I had to use those thoughts then to improve my game. You get on in sport by upping your game, not waiting for someone else's game to fail. That's the way I've always looked at it.

DB Did it have that effect then?

NO I think it did. That World Cup moved me up the rankings, certainly.

DB Did you get any feedback on your performances at the World Cup? You probably did, more than I did at my first one!

NO Yes I did. I had a phone call and I asked whether I'd been in the mix. I was told that my name had been discussed for the quarters, but they decided against appointing me that year. I was then told that it was only a matter of time, and to concentrate on my game and work up the ranks, as it were. I was told that my goal should be to get a few of the big Six Nations games. The following year that happened, when I had France Ireland and Italy Scotland.

I was told something that I'll never forget by Rob Yemen, the referees' manager. He told me that it was often not the best thing to wish for a particular game. The rugby version of 'be careful what you wish for', I suppose. How right he was!

DB Because of Mr Barnes' performance in the game between France and New Zealand?

NO Exactly that! It wasn't a game without its controversies, and, because of that one infamous incident involving a forward pass, it knocked Wayne's career off-track for a good while. New Zealand were knocked out by France, 18–20, causing Richie McCaw and the whole of New Zealand to criticise the IRB for choosing 'the most inexperienced referee on the roster' and accusing him of being 'frozen with fear and wouldn't make any big calls'.

DB It didn't help that there was one specific incident either did it, when Wayne was alleged to have missed that forward pass in a move that led to France's second try. The All Blacks felt that the game, the occasion, deserved a more experienced ref.

NO It was a very important lesson for me to learn early on that, like everything in life, you need a bit of luck sometimes. Refereeing is no different. There was another change that year in the World Cup that meant the tournament moved forward quite a bit. That's the year, as far as refs are concerned, that things stepped-up a notch or two in terms of being professional. Lots of refs had complained, in 2003 for example, that they had to do fitness routines on arrival in Australia after long-haul flights, at other inconvenient times and in inconvenient circumstances. There was one story of having to do a speed test but the track given to them wasn't long enough and they had to carry on past the end of it, round a Coca-Cola vending machine, and back again. That kind of thing. In fact, a couple of referees pulled up injured in that fitness testing in 2003. Things were a lot sharper in 2007.

Another difference that year, compared to the later ones in my experience, was the fact that it was in France. I didn't understand the French language so I couldn't read anything about the games in the papers or listen to anything on TV or radio. Also, the public perception of rugby in Paris itself isn't the same as it is in New Zealand for example, or Wales of course. It's such a massive city and not a rugby city at all.

The rugby hotbed areas are in the South of France. So it was easy not to know that there was a World Cup going on in the capital. These two things meant a lot less pressure. You were very lucky if you saw fans walking past, and no one would recognise you if you sat outside having a coffee. Things might be a little different on an actual match day at the Stade de France, but even then, nothing like Cardiff on a match day.

DB No chance of that happening now with you Nige, not even in France!

NO Maybe not! It was so different in New Zealand in 2011, so much more intense, more of a cauldron, with no hiding place. The same was true in London in 2015 as well. But in my case, after 2007, I had to get to a position to be selected for New Zealand 2011 first, and that wasn't a straightforward journey at all. It started well enough, and for about a year after the 2007 tournament things were going really well. But then I hit a patch of bad form and had to work hard to make sure I was even going to go the World Cup.

DB And, of course, if you knew things weren't right, then so too did Paddy O'Brien, the referees' manager.

NO Of course he did! He spoke to me quite clearly, telling

Derek was fitter as a referee than he ever was as a player

Nigel keeping a France game running smoothly

me that I might well end up going to the World Cup but, as things were, it wasn't very likely that I would be going as one of the leading referees. He told me in no uncertain terms to buck up my ideas. That was quite a shaking, especially as I remembered the chat with him when he told me that I was in the mix for the next stage in my previous World Cup. It felt as if I'd gone down from there, which is the opposite direction to the one I should have been going in. But, in the end, luckily, I did enough to get to the 2011 World Cup.

DB But what kind of fixtures did you have? They probably reflected the way things had been for you in the lead-up to the finals.

NO They certainly did. My first game was Fiji Namibia. Then Japan New Zealand, followed by Australia USA, and the fourth was my only big game, South Africa Samoa. That's always been a horrible game to referee in a World Cup, so getting it wasn't a gift of any sort. The first three games went very well, thank goodness. The fourth was OK. I did a decent job, even though there were a few things I could have done better.

DB I'm sure it was absolutely no comfort at all at the time, but we all need those lean patches. There's a lot to learn from them.

NO It's easy to get too complacent, yes it is. But you have to be careful when you get a really good patch as well. The temptation then is to feel almost untouchable. As soon as that happens, that's when you're prone to dropping your guard a bit; things start to go not so well. That's when you need a good kick up the backside. That's what I had in the run-up to the 2011 World Cup and at the tournament itself. Because those four games went as well as they did, I was thankfully given a quarter-final match. What a relief that was. I was chosen for the New Zealand Argentina game. Anyway Bev, back to you, what about reffing the final itself then, in your second World Cup?

DB It's hard to believe now but, between the end of the 1987 World Cup and the beginning of the 1991 tournament, I had only refereed five international matches! One of those was the Bledisloe Cup right after the World Cup. But the point is, that didn't matter so much then. As you were picked for international duty by your own home union, it was more important that you had plenty of club games and that you performed well at home. As in 1987, there were three Welshmen in contention for two World Cup refereeing places for 1991. Clive Norling was again one of them, along with Les Peard and myself. The one change that had just been introduced in Wales, not long before the World Cup, was that Ken Rowlands had been appointed as the first ever full-time Director of Referees in Wales. So things were changing for rugby officials too.

That year, the two semi-finals and the final of the Welsh Cup were shared out between us. Clive and I did the semis and Les had the final. The three of us had a chance to prove ourselves therefore, and stake our claim for selection.

To cut a long story short, Clive had the raw deal this time. He wasn't picked to go to the World Cup at all. He ended up commentating on the tournament for ITV.

NO That must have been really hard for him to take.

DB It was, without doubt. I think it hit him more than he showed. So it was Les and me for the 1991 tournament.

Derek at the 1999 Welsh Cup, with fellow officials Les Peard, Clive Norling and Gareth Simmonds

NO Wasn't he the one involved in some landmark game as far as a refereeing law was concerned?

DB Yes he was Nige, you're right. He was the ref in the 1990 Welsh Cup final I just mentioned, between Neath and Bridgend. He gave Neath's Mark Jones a yellow card which meant he was off the pitch for ten minutes – that was the first time the sin-bin had been used. If you're going to go, you might as well go in the final I suppose! So that's Mark's claim to fame and Les' of course! And then the World Cup comes to town. It was a significant year, not just because it was the first up here in the Northern Hemisphere, but because new countries were invited to be there. As well as the usual main rugby playing nations, Romania, Japan, the USA and Zimbabwe were there too. This meant that officials from those countries were there as well.

NO Just to pick up on the yellow card theme, Bev. I have something in common with Les then, as I was involved in a yellow card first as well. I was the first ref to issue a yellow card. That was in a match between Trebanos and Trimsaran. There was no sin-bin then, it hadn't been introduced, just the showing of a card as an official warning. I might well not have been the first if the match hadn't been moved from the Saturday kick-off to the Friday night before. I had a bit of a head-start on all the other refs in that case! Then, in my final in 2015, there was another yellow card first, the first in a World Cup final, with sin-bin this time of course! Not the main thing you want to be remembered for, but it's there in the history books and, in Les' case as in mine, I'm sure it had to be done.

I suppose the presence of the Tier 2 countries was a big indication of how the game was growing at that time, and it's a growth we've seen ever since then really. It must have been a big step-up for the officials from the new countries.

DB There was still no one there from South Africa mind, player or official, as they were still banned from sporting events because of apartheid. They didn't turn up for a World Cup until 1995, which they hosted and won.

NO That was the first tournament to be held in one country only as well – and we had a Clint Eastwood film, *Invictus*, out of it!

DB Anyway, back to 1991. The presence of the emerging rugby nations brings to mind two particular stories. The more experienced refs were given a referee from the new countries to look after and guide through the tournament. I was given a Japanese man we called Yagi-San. I'll never forget him receiving his official kit, which was about six sizes too big for him! The top of his socks could go under his shorts. There was no such thing as tailor-made then, obviously. The other story was a little more, well, sad in a way. That year, tournament officials were given bed and breakfast, including getting our laundry done. We also had a £50 a day allowance. When the Romanian ref received his envelope with the first 14 days' allowance in it, he was completely overwhelmed! I watched him look at the pile of notes and count them again and again in disbelief. It was more than he had ever seen in one go in his life and, as he said, enough to buy him a flat in Communist Romania. And then he started to tell stories of how he remembered phoning his wife at home and hearing gunfire in the background. It really did make you think.

NO That's quite something, I must say. And it was the ref's pocket money that had that effect on him. I presume that it was the refs from the emerging nations who were sent home first, after the pool stages?

DB Yes it was, but we also knew that a few of the top-tier refs would have to go home as well. So we weren't guaranteed anything. The irony for me was that my chances of progressing further into the competition increased greatly when Wales were knocked out. Their failure meant a greater possibility of success for me. That's a strange situation to be in, when you think of balancing your love for your country with your personal ambition. We were assessed on ten different aspects of our performances in that tournament, with each ref being given an overall score. The assessment criterion was better than it was in 1987; it was a little tighter, but still it was basically the same system.

NO Were you given a third-party phone message over dinner this time then?

DB No, luckily! We were called together for a meeting, with the names of the twelve staying read out, leaving the two not mentioned to get the message that they were to go home. As the names were called out in alphabetical order, I knew straightaway that I was chosen! I was thrilled. But the edge was taken off that a bit when I realised that Les was one of the two who would be going home, along with Patrick Robin from France. I was gutted for Les. But there was a twist in the tale. The Frenchman who had been chosen, René Hourquet, thought that some of those chosen to continue weren't fit enough to do so and that it was wrong that Robin had not been selected. He made his point in a very dramatic way. He turned up to dinner one evening, covered in bandages and plasters and his arm in a sling, and declared to everyone that he was fully fit to officiate in the Rugby World Cup! You can imagine how that went down. He was criticising some of his fellow officials. Arguments dragged on throughout the dinner and into the night.

Referees' solidarity was being tested for the very first time. In the end, after a very acrimonious gathering of the refs, Hourquet decided that he couldn't stay if Robin wasn't, and he pulled out of the tournament. Les was chosen instead of him. That wasn't a good situation and we were all unhappy as to how the whole incident started and then escalated.

NO That's not a very subtle or considerate way to make your point, is it! So in the first year of the first full-time Director of Refereeing, there were two Welshmen in the knockout stages. That was a good start. So what happened when the officials for the 1991 semi-finals were announced? That's usually a significant occasion.

DB Indeed it is, because you know that if you're chosen for the semis you're not going to referee the final. I wasn't chosen for the semis! Well, as you can imagine, it's hard to contain your expectations in such circumstances. There was only one thing for me to do. Go home! As the tournament was 'local', I could go home easily enough. I watched the semi-final matches, between New Zealand and Australia and Scotland against England, in my home rugby club, Vardre. My fellow World Cup referee, Australian Sandy MacNeill, was with me, having come to stay at my house for the semis weekend. We had a great time and, I must say, Vardre did him proud!

The following Tuesday, with nothing announced about who would be reffing the final, I went for a jog in Cardiff with the other Australian referee, Kerry Fitzgerald, the man who had refereed the first ever World Cup final in 1987. When we got back to the hotel, The Angel, Ken Rowlands from the WRU was in the foyer, grinning like a Cheshire cat but saying nothing. Not long afterwards I was told the best news ever. The final was mine! The boy from Vardre was in charge of the World Cup final. It was an amazing feeling. Ken Rowlands was so emotional. He hugged me and had to turn away because he was so overwhelmed. It was, of course, an honour for him as it was his full-time job to develop referees and refereeing in Wales. Kerry too was very excited for me. He grabbed hold of me to congratulate me and then added, 'I'm so glad! I've grown a little fed up of being called "The Rugby World Cup Final Referee". At least now there are two of us!'

NO I can certainly identify with your response, but by replacing Vardre with Mynyddcerrig of course! I was really moved by the people of my home village putting up a banner across the street, with a message of congratulations, when I was chosen to referee the 2015 final. That was real and very meaningful for me. That's what counts at the end of the day, that's what's important, your roots.

DB I couldn't agree more, Nige. It was easy to lose sight of that in the run-up to the final. It was such a busy time, with a mix of preparation and frantic media activity taking up every waking hour. I enjoyed the media attention at first, but I soon got to the point when I asked the hotel receptionist to block all my calls. I didn't have time to think and that wasn't good. The messages of support were unbelievable. So many came from people I didn't know, including stars from other sports. But I must say that it's the Vardre boys who gave me the best message: 'Make sure those English bastards don't win it!'

Derek's official portrait as a referee at the 1991 rugby World Cup finals

NO That's certainly taking the traditional English Welsh banter a step further! What were your thoughts as you walked out onto the pitch for that final?

DB When the day of the final came, a match between England and Australia at Twickenham, it was quite an emotional occasion, if not a little tense. The Queen and the Prime Minister met players and officials before the game.

But when the ceremonial meet and greet was over, I took my place on the halfway line for the kick-off. Despite the fact that there were tens of thousands of people in the stadium, despite the fact that two of the world's top teams were on the pitch ready for the biggest occasion in rugby for four years, my thoughts went to one person only. My dad. He had passed away and wouldn't be able to share this experience with me. I remembered how he laughed when I told him I wanted to be a referee, because he knew that I'd been sent off more than once as a player! And then I blew the whistle for the start of the final.

NO I was in a similar position, Bev. My mum was still alive when I got to my first World Cup finals, but had passed away by the time I got to referee the final itself. Not that she could ever watch me refereeing live, mind you. There was no chance of that as she would get far too nervous. She would rarely watch me on TV, either. She didn't like people shouting at me and calling me names. All that changed, however, during what proved to be the last year of her life. She watched every single game I refereed if it was broadcast live on TV. That would have been in 2008, which was a good year for me as the man in the middle. It was as if I knew I had to do it for her, as she wouldn't be around for much longer to share in my achievements.

When it then came to the 2015 final, my thoughts were with my family too. Whatever the occasion, your mind is always pulled back to what's really central to your life. My mother wasn't around to see me reffing my World Cup final, and that was in my thoughts, no doubt about that. Knowing how to react to that, to put it into perspective, was a bit of a job I must say.

DB I had to put my personal thoughts behind me once the match got under way. It went very well from my point of view, although it wasn't a classic of a match by any stretch of the imagination. Australia won by 12 points to 6, scoring the only try of the game. Afterwards I was totally knackered and just wanted to go to bed. I forced my way through the after-match celebrations, drained to say the least. Luckily, there weren't any big controversies in the game, apart from my not allowing England a penalty try when David Campese had deliberately knocked-on with England close to crossing the line! I was happy that there was sufficient cover not to award the penalty try, and I awarded a penalty only. It was an issue that was analysed intensely after the game. But, luckily, most people agreed with my interpretation. Maybe Campese didn't though!

NO I didn't have any issues like that, thankfully, in my final at Twickenham in 2015. If the tournament in France was a good one for me to start in, because of the relative anonymity of the game and the tournament itself in that country, then I must say that, of the three World Cups I've done, the best location for me to referee a final was the one I did, at Twickenham. That's because it was on the same time zone as back home, and my dad and all my friends and family were able to be in the club in Mynyddcerrig to watch the game. They wouldn't be in the clubhouse if the final I reffed had been in New Zealand, for example. That might sound like something small, but it really isn't. It was a big part of the occasion, knowing that they were all there in the clubhouse in my home village at the same time as I was officiating at Twickenham. Not only for those in the clubhouse, but for the village as a whole as well. I was lucky in that sense. There was a big difference in the home reaction to the 2015 final as compared to the first World Cup I ever officiated in. It was relatively low-key the first time round. There was a big fuss in the family of course and with close friends, but not in the village as a whole. It couldn't have been more different in 2015!

At the final, as I was standing on the pitch just before the start of the game, a vivid picture came into my head. It was an impossible one, but it showed how I was thinking and feeling. I pictured myself back in the clubhouse in Mynyddcerrig, with everyone else who had squeezed into it to watch the match, including my dad, sharing that moment with them, watching myself refereeing the World Cup final.

DB What about the run-up to your final then, Nige? How did things come together for you?

NO I had a really great experience in the run-up to the final.

In the final game of Pool D, France were playing Ireland at Cardiff. It was a good game and it was something quite special to referee a World Cup match in my home stadium. After that game, it was back to London to our tournament HQ and then a Monday morning official meeting of all the refs in the tournament, as happened every week. A little bit like with you Bev, we knew that if we weren't in the semis we stood a good chance of getting the final. The slight twist for us was that it was also true that if you were chosen for the quarter-finals you knew that you were one of the four referees in the mix for the final. I suppose there were about six of us in contention for those four games: Joubert, Barnes, Garcès and myself, with Poite and Peyper as outside chances.

DB Jérôme Garcès was reffing very well at that time. He's certainly the best French referee I've seen.

NO That's right. When I was chosen to referee one of the quarter-finals, I then knew that if I performed well in the game I was in with a really good shout for the final. And what a quarter-final I was given! It was the game between New Zealand and France. I didn't think I would get that one as I'd reffed France Ireland the week before. You don't usually get the same team two games running. Of the four quarters, it was the big one. But it ended up as mine.

There had been issues between these two teams in the previous two World Cups. In 2007 New Zealand lost the

The referees' team for the 2015 Rugby World Cup final. Nigel with assistant referees Jérôme Garcès, Wayne Barnes and Jaco Peyper and TMO Shaun Veldsman.

Derek at the Bermuda World Rugby Classic

game because of the officials missing a forward pass. In the final in 2011, New Zealand won, but the French fans gave the ref, Joubert, a little bit of stick for his performance.

DB You're being very kind when you say a little bit of stick!

NO So in the previous two World Cups, there had been issues between the French, the New Zealanders and the match officials. This fixture was fast becoming the kiss of death for us refs! That was very much on my mind as I approached my 2015 quarter-final between the two countries. I had one clear thought in my mind as I prepared for that game: there was absolutely no way that I was going to let this game become a talking point about me! I was going to referee out of my skin.

Luckily for me, New Zealand played their best rugby of that World Cup in that game and easily beat France 62–13, with Julian Savea scoring a hat-trick. It was a brilliant game of rugby in terms of skill level and the playing of an open game. France contributed to that, too. Even if I made any mistakes in such a game, no one would be talking about them.

That weekend I was again reminded of the point I mentioned previously, about being careful which games you wish for as a ref. I've always maintained that I will never pick a game which I would prefer to referee, and one of the other quarter-finals reminded me of that loud and clear.

DB Ah, you mean the controversial encounter between Australia and Scotland. I remember that. Poor Joubert, caught up in another argument about a decision. Scotland were winning with six or seven minutes left. They were looking at a historic place in the semi-final of the World Cup. Just before the end, Joubert gives Australia a penalty; it's kicked by Bernard Foley and Australia have the lead which they hang on to for the few minutes until the end of the game. Problem was, no one thought the Scotland player penalised for being offside was actually offside. TV replays seemed to suggest that they were right and the decision was wrong. Scotland were denied a semi-final. I felt so sorry for them.

NO That was really tough on them. But, prior to the quarter-finals, I'd been thinking that the Scotland Australia game would have been the least complicated of the four to referee. I was so wrong, and lucky not to have been in charge of that game.

DB You can't really think like that, because you probably wouldn't have made that decision! And you certainly wouldn't have run off the pitch at the end of the game like he did without talking to anyone. He made a fool of himself that day.

Anyway, back to you and your game! I was in the clubhouse in Vardre and, over a pint, I told the boys, 'You watch, Nigel will get New Zealand France'. My thinking was this. There was no way they were going to give it to Joubert after his decision cost France the game in the previous finals, especially as the man in charge of selection was a Frenchman! Now, you can't say that Nigel, but I can! I didn't think there was any way they could give it to Barnes either, because he was the man in charge during the France New Zealand controversy in the finals before last. Nigel will get it, I said, not by default but because he deserves it and that will then be his doorway to reffing the final itself.

NO The atmosphere in that Monday morning refs' meeting was very difficult. We all felt for Joubert, as it was the kind of mistake any of us could have made. We all supported him as much as we could, as that's what we do as refs when any one of us has one of those controversial games or decisions. We all know how lonely games like that can make you feel.

After a short debrief, it was time to move on and think about the games ahead. We had ended up with the first ever all Southern Hemisphere semi-finals, South Africa, Argentina, Australia and New Zealand.

Glen Jackson and John Lacey were sat next to me, two of my best friends in refereeing. The officials for the semis were announced and I wasn't given any role in either game. Glen turned to me and said, 'Congratulations Nige!' I looked daft at him and replied, 'What are you on about? I haven't got a f***ing game!' 'No, because the final's yours,' was his short response.

That's a difficult thing to respond to! I had huge respect

for Glen and he wouldn't make such a comment lightly. I also knew that, in that World Cup to date, things had gone very well for me and I'd made no major errors. But the other voices in my head were telling me, 'Until you're told, you don't know.' There were also feelings of relief that I hadn't been chosen for a semi, as well as feeling sorry for Wayne Barnes because I know he would have loved to referee a World Cup final in his home country – who wouldn't? Being chosen for the semis was the end of that aspiration, especially with me not having been given a semi. It was a bit of an emotional rollercoaster to say the least.

DB I suppose you found out about your final at the Monday meeting after the semis?

NO Officially, yes. There had been rumours all week, but nothing official. At that meeting I was told officially. My response was a strange one. It was more relief than elation. Relief that all the tension created by the speculation, the guessing, the suggestions, was now over. I could now relax – apart from the fact, of course, that I now had a World Cup final to prepare for!

DB It's a hell of a long wait, waiting for the day of the final to arrive, and then when it does it's 80 minutes of play and it's all over. The chances are that you won't get the opportunity to do it again, so the best thing to do is to enjoy it, to embrace it. But before that Nige, you had a special event on the Tuesday after being told, didn't you?

NO Yes, I certainly did. I was in the referees' room, starting my preparation for the final. I watched some videos, looking at scrummaging I think. Then I played cards with some of the others. I remember thinking that there seemed to be a hell of a lot of refs still hanging around the room. That was unusual, as they would have all gone home by then. Joël Jutge, the Head of Refs, called us together, saying he wanted to show us something. It was a video compilation of good luck messages from former World Cup final refs Alain Rolland and Craig Joubert, Warren Gatland, referees' manager Nigel Whitehouse, and many others as well. Then, cue Mr Bevan's video contribution! What did you say, Bev?

Getting ready for play – Nigel about to referee the New Zealand v Barbarians fixture for the first time, at Twickenham

DB 'Nige, we've got a lot in common,' I said. 'I was 44 years of age when I reffed my final, you're 44 reffing yours. We both come from small villages in west Wales. Thirdly, we both refereed a World Cup final at Twickenham, and fourth, Australia was involved in my World Cup final and they're involved in yours.' I then finished by adding, 'The only difference between us is our sexuality!'

NO Everyone in the room was rolling around laughing at that! I certainly had tears in my eyes. Only Bev!

2

Two Tales

NO The actual one event that sent me headlong into refereeing has been well documented. It's in the first part of my autobiography, *Half Time*, and I've said the story on TV, radio, in the newspapers and during speaking engagements. Basically, I missed a crucial kick in front of the posts, denying my school team victory. The teachers' suggestion for me to take up refereeing was therefore a not-so-subtle comment on the fact that I obviously wasn't good enough to play the game! All that is true, of course. But the seeds of refereeing had been sown in my mind a good four or five years before that disastrous game. And that story is very much a part of the roots of the world I was born into. There was certainly no ambition on my part to be a referee. That's never something that I said as a young boy or later as a teenager.

I was born in the Gwendraeth Valley. Anthracite country in days gone by, the best coal of its type in the world, so they said. That's gone now, unfortunately. But it was there when I was born. That part of Carmarthenshire was a mix of mining and farming when I came into this world, with both industries shaping whole villages and communities, and its people feeling the pull of both. Part of that shaping was the game of rugby. And if coal has gone, rugby certainly hasn't!

As soon as I was born, it was there, all around me. I picked up a rugby ball at six years of age. I'd just watched Scotland against Wales at the Five Nations, the game where Phil Bennett scored an amazing try, wonderfully described by the unique Bill McLaren. I played on the streets, in school like everybody else, just as in so many other villages across south Wales of course. I wasn't that brilliant a player I must say, but I played. Soon, as I entered my teenage years, I started going with my father on a Saturday to watch village team Tumble play. It wasn't my nearest village team. But there were links that pulled us there. My first cousin, Phil Owens, was a regular on the wing for Tumble during a period when they were without doubt the best team in west Wales. Another father and son from Mynyddcerrig, Cyril and Robert Owen, had started going to Tumble too to watch the rugby.

Tumble has a long tradition of being a first-class village team, with links to famous rugby names such as Barry John and Dwayne Peel. British Lion Gareth Davies is also a native of Tumble. Those, whose names didn't mean much outside the village or beyond the west Wales rugby community, were certainly heroes in their area: players such as Tonto Arwel and Gareth Davies and the late Peris Williams, to name but a few. It was a big thing for me as a ten year old to go and watch them. I don't say for one minute that I watched every second of each game. We used to play behind the goalposts as a gang of boys, occasionally turning our attention to what was happening on the pitch. Soon I started to meet one or two of the players, the men who I had heard other men talk about in such admiring terms. After the home games I would go into the clubhouse with everyone else. This led to me meeting some of the team members. I'll never forget the day when one of them, the legend called Tonto, gave me his meal voucher so that I could have his curry and chips! Amazing! I could live off that story for weeks to come with all the boys at school!

As this went on I remember that after one game, a Cup game I think, Clive Norling was back in the clubhouse with everybody else. I watched him eagerly as people went up to him to shake his hand and have a chat with him. I could see that he was a definite presence in that clubhouse and not just because he was big! On that occasion I remember some of the Tumble players talking about Norling and saying how good a ref he was. Then Robert Owen, from Mynyddcerrig, turned to me and said, 'There you are Nigel, if you don't turn out to be a good player, you can always become a ref!'

When he said that I didn't take it as being something derogatory at all. They said that Clive wasn't that good a player but he had turned out to be a first-class referee. I took the comment as saying that that was a course that might be open to me. But I left those thoughts there that day, and didn't think any more about the whole issue.

And then, when that fateful day came, those comments were resurrected. We'd had a particularly bad season that year when I was in Form 5 at Maes-yr-Yrfa School (called Year 11 now of course). In fact, we hadn't won a single game. The school was relatively small because it was a Welsh comprehensive school set up after the abolition of the grammar school system, and it could be a bit of a job to get a whole team together. That was great news for average players like me. It meant that we were likely to get a game or two. That's what happened in this particular game against Ysgol Griffith Jones, a comprehensive school in St Clears, just outside Carmarthen. I was picked as full-back. Miraculously, we scored a late try through one of my best friends at the school, Wayne Thomas. The match was now level at 12–12. A successful conversion kick would give us a rare victory. Our captain, Craig, was another good friend of mine and I told him that I would take the conversion, no doubt sensing glory! It wasn't a difficult kick but I hit the ball wrongly and it sailed towards the touchline instead of towards the posts that were right in front of me. To make matters worse, the school's Year 7 team, whose game had finished, had come to watch our match because it was such a close, engaging game. So they too saw my failed kick and, with that, a failure to win our first game of the season. Needless to say, my fellow Year 11 boys and the on-looking Year 7 boys gave me a hard time for a good long while after that. Craig didn't speak to me for weeks! It's still known to crop up in occasional bar banter to this day!

My PE teacher's response is the one that's usually referred to when the beginning of my career is discussed. John Beynon was a huge influence on me and so many other pupils in his care. He was an inspirational man. I let him down too that day. After my failed kick, he came up to me with a broad smile on his face, and asked if I had ever considered being a referee as I obviously couldn't play the game. So a few days later I offered to referee a few inter-house school games. He then put me in charge of a few school matches he had organised, which was an invaluable start for me.

Soon after that another teacher, James Rees, came up to me and showed me a poster. It was a mock-up of the old First World War poster showing Lord Kitchener pointing his finger and saying 'Your Country Needs You'. Except, of course, this wasn't about war, but the Welsh Rugby Union looking for people to become referees – which is its own kind of war, I suppose!

So with the words of John Beynon and the actions of James Rees, thoughts of Tumble Rugby Club came flooding back. Hadn't I already been told that, if I wasn't good enough to play, refereeing was an option? And wasn't I told that by some of the boys who were my local heroes on the pitch? The trigger for these comments was the presence of Clive Norling in the clubhouse after a match. I had seen how everyone there was responding to him. It all looked good to me!

John Beynon's words didn't fall onto a blank page then.

And with his encouragement and James Rees showing me that poster, there were specific, practical things that I could do in order to become a referee. I was on the path!

DB My story starts in a very similar way to Nigel's, even if the era might be a little different! It also starts with coal, family influences, a community and local grassroots rugby, just like Nigel. But, unlike Nigel, I went to work underground myself. I followed my two brothers to the coalface, with our father having been there before us. I worked at the Brynlliw Colliery near Gorseinon. It was hard work; it was potentially dangerous but I loved it. I was an electrician, responsible for keeping the machinery that cut the coal at the face, the plough system, and the conveyor belt that then carried the coal to the surface, in fine working order. Failure to do so would mean a break in production and all that meant in terms of productivity and profit.

When I wasn't working hard I was playing hard for Vardre RFC, my home team, captaining the club for a while too. I was born in Clydach and I still live there. Roots are important to me. That's another thing that Nigel and I have in common. I was a flanker, settling in that position eventually after having tried a few others before that. I loved the game of rugby. I loved taking my place on the pitch with other boys from the village. I loved what rugby gave as a contact sport and I loved the connections it gave me off the pitch as well: the clubhouse banter, social networking, and community spirit, call it what you may. It was central to life itself.

And then, one day, my life fell apart. I was at work in a part of the coalface where it wasn't possible to stand up. I was on my hands and knees, fixing an electrical fault, when I heard a rumbling noise that was quite unnerving. It was followed by the sound of a loud cracking, then the thunderous noise of the coal above me breaking and falling. I was trapped. I couldn't move a muscle. There was no room to panic even. Luckily, my colleagues were close at hand and they rushed over to me. Carefully, they freed me and took me to the surface. That was in 1972 and I was 25.

It being an accident at work, I had to go and see a hospital specialist. He told me that recovery would take a full two years and that I was to avoid contact sport at all costs. My initial response was one of relief that recovery was possible. I had feared that it wasn't. Relief at being alive was then replaced by a fear that I would be paralysed, to whatever degree, for the rest of my life. To hear that recovery was possible, therefore, was a triple blessing.

I knew that would mean giving up playing rugby for those two years. But that was OK. I could still play my part in the life of Vardre Rugby Club by being on the committee. I could organise events, help to look after the pitch, sell raffle tickets, and all that being a committee member entails. I did all that and more for a while. But I hated it. It was really difficult to work behind the bar on match days and hear the players coming in after a game and talking enthusiastically about the match they'd just played. I felt left out. I was missing what used to be.

At the time, the chairman of Vardre Rugby Club, Evan Dan, had a word with me. He suggested that I should think about refereeing. That, he said, would still keep me involved with the game on match day, but without the contact. I knew he had been a referee himself at some stage. But I didn't take the suggestion very well! I laughed in his face, telling him that I couldn't stand refs! I also knew that the reason I liked rugby was that it was a team game. The thought of going to matches on my own left me cold.

Many others thought the idea laughable too, all only too keen to point out that I'd been sent off twice, officially, during my playing career, with a third sending off having been explained away by some clever use of smoke and mirrors! How could a player with such a record be a referee? That was the question, if not the accusation, when people heard I was thinking of being the man in the middle.

There was a huge shortage of referees in those days. Anyone who showed the slightest interest would have been welcomed with open arms and a whistle thrown in their direction straightaway. It wasn't something that any youngster would even consider. I had a good illustration of this in one of the early games I refereed. When I got to the club, the committeeman showed me the way to the visitors' dressing room. When I told him I was the ref, there was a look of total disbelief on his face. 'How come someone as young as you is a ref, then?' I was 26. He then followed that up with, 'You can't have been any good as a player, obviously!'

But for me, I realised that it actually was an ideal solution. I threw myself into it with gusto, while at the same time reminding everyone that it would only be for two years and then I'd be back playing. So, as with Nigel, my involvement with refereeing came directly from my playing the game of rugby. Except, with me, I didn't turn to reffing because I wasn't a good enough player but because I wasn't allowed to play any more. That's another case of where Nige and I differ!

I started with local teams. But there was one problem. I hadn't learnt the laws. I wasn't very aware of them when I played the game and, when I started reffing, some of the players knew the laws much better than me! So it was a case of bluffing my way through, being assertive even if I didn't know what I was being assertive about. It seemed to work. I got to the stage, though, when more formal instruction was needed. I went on a course run by Gwyn Watts, the PE teacher at Bishop Gore School in Swansea. For three weeks I went twice a week to his course and I learned so much! The pass target at the end of the course was 90 per cent. I got 98 per cent. Maybe I was cut out to be a referee after all!

I knew that I had to follow that up with working on my fitness. I started to go running several times a week and, in the end, I was fitter as a ref than I'd ever been as a player. Maybe being faced with the injuries the accident gave me, and thinking about what could have happened, made me think more about staying fit and healthy.

My reffing career soon took hold and I saw how difficult it would be to referee in an atmosphere as close-knit as it is in south Wales' rugby communities. It wasn't long before I came face to face in confrontation with someone from my own home club. Nothing emphasised the culture I came from more than that early encounter.

I was given the Aberavon versus Llanelli fixture this particular season. A Vardre boy, Carl Yates, had been chosen to play his first game for Aberavon. On hearing that I was to referee that game, the boys in the club said, 'Oh Bev, you're

Derek orchestrating a scrum

reffing that game are you? You know who's playing prop don't you? Carl!' I had played with his father for Vardre. So, of course, his debut for Aberavon was a big event. His family were all there. There was a minibus from the village. It was a big occasion. As the game went on, Llanelli were pulling away comfortably, so Aberavon naturally tried to slow the game down which inevitably meant things boiled over now and again. I called some players together and said that my patience was running out. 'Next incident,' I said, 'there's going to be trouble, just play the game.' Not long after, a scrum broke down and a fight followed. Carl Yates and the Llanelli prop, Anthony Buchanan, were having a right old fist fight. I stood between them and said, 'If you stop now, you'll stay on the pitch.' Buchanan dropped his arms and gave in. And then Carl threw a punch at him! There was absolutely no choice for me. Carl had to be sent off! I could see the Vardre boys on the side of the pitch. I could see Carl's family. They were all really unhappy to say the least! Carl never let me forget that incident and his mum didn't speak to me for over six months after that. I got the message loud and clear that day: Welsh rugby is played in goldfish bowl.

But, I had chosen my path and I was enjoying it. An accident at work had not only changed my involvement with rugby but ended up changing my whole life too.

3

Tales of
the First Steps

DB If your experiences in the World Cup were different to mine Nige, I'm pretty sure that the early days of my reffing, when I first picked up the whistle, were in another age compared to yours! I started reffing in the Swansea District League.

NO My beginnings were in District as well of course, but I'm intrigued how your attitude to the rules of the game changed when you moved from player to ref.

DB Well, as one who had been sent off twice officially and a third time unofficially, they had to! I suppose that I learned pretty early on as a young ref that rugby is governed by laws not rules. Laws are laws and that's it. Rules however, as my playing days showed, are there to be broken!

NO I didn't have the same dilemma as you, having to leave playing for a team – and a team I'd captained too – and then turn to reffing. That can't have been easy.

DB It wasn't. OK, I knew that I didn't have a choice because of my injury. But it was still very difficult to let go. After any game I would be reffing on a Saturday, I would go back to Vardre Rugby Club immediately to be a part of the after-game atmosphere. The league changes at the time in our region favoured Vardre and we started to do very well, which made it worse for me as I missed out on some really good games because I was away reffing somewhere or other. Vardre had a good Cup run, for example, which I missed out on. We played Bridgend, Newport and Pontypool, which I missed because I was away somewhere or other. So that bit wasn't easy at all, I must say.

NO With your playing record, it must have been an interesting moment when you sent off your first player!

DB Poacher turned gamekeeper you mean! I remember it well! It was a game in Penclawdd, and a youth Cup game at that! To make matters a lot worse, the one I sent off, Richard Jones, was due to have a Welsh trial the following week. Because I showed him the red card, he was banned and wasn't allowed to play in the trial. Well, you can imagine the response of Penclawdd Rugby Club members. They took me apart! That was my first experience of dissent from club officials and it was very uncomfortable. I was due to be paid six shillings – 30 pence in today's money! The treasurer came into the dressing room with the money and threw it on the floor, coins scattering everywhere! His parting shot was a slightly more impolite way of saying that he hoped he never saw me again!

Thankfully, at the next district meeting of referees, I was to learn that this was a common occurrence – the dissent of club officials – and that it was something I should get used to. It was good to get their support.

NO I remember my first district rugby union referees' society meeting! It was at Furnace Rugby Club in Llanelli. I was taken there by the guy whose parents ran the Post Office in my home village, Mynyddcerrig. Alan Rees, Y Post, was also a rugby referee. I hadn't reffed a game at that point, apart from at Maes-yr-Yrfa School, but he took me along as part of my learning curve. At that meeting I received my first copy of the laws of the game. I also ended up being given my first game outside Maes-yr-Yrfa School fixtures. I was asked to referee Carmarthenshire Schools versus Pembrokeshire Schools in Carmarthen. I think of that game every time I pass the big Tesco superstore on the edge of town, because the game was played on the rugby fields there before the supermarket was built. It's a little sad to think that the fields where I refereed my first ever game are no longer there. The game went well for me personally, and I caught the eye of one or two key individuals.

DB So where does that poster the teacher showed you come into this then, Nige? Your country needs you and all that!

NO That didn't turn out as planned, unfortunately. After seeing the poster I applied for the ref recruiting programme it was advertising, but I was told that I had to be 18. I was gutted. I was only 16. To make things worse, I had no hope of getting anywhere with WRU reffing until I did that course. It was a setback right at the start. However, I was allowed to do local games under the guidance of the Llanelli and District Referees' body, with Alun West, the fixtures secretary, keeping a watchful eye over me. That's where I had to start. That's how I ended up at that meeting in Furnace Rugby Club.

DB Being 16, you faced practical difficulties to get around the district to referee your games I would assume. How did you manage that?

NO That definitely was an issue. I obviously couldn't drive. My dad didn't like to drive long distances and had never even driven round a roundabout. So him taking me further than the Gwendraeth Valley was not an option. Public transport was the other option, which was hardly an option at all really! For some fixtures I would have had to leave on Friday and get back home on Sunday! So it was down to my Uncle Ken to be my chauffeur! He took me to all the games he could. I made the referees' society aware of my situation, but it didn't seem to register. The next game they gave me was in Tregaron! Could hardly have been worse. Well, actually, it did get worse because my Uncle Ken wasn't available that day. Luckily, Tregaron's opposition was Nantgaredig. The fixtures secretary, Alun West, who had appointed me to the game, suggested that if I could get to Nantgaredig, then he would arrange for me to go on the bus with them from there. The club said that they were happy for me to travel up with them on the team bus. Sorted.

DB That's a twist on an impartial ref, isn't it?! How did that go down?

NO I was so afraid of the reaction when I got to Tregaron that I climbed out of the back window of the bus so that no one could see me arriving with the away team! I got away with it. Until, that is, it was time to go home. In the clubhouse after the game, one of the Nantgaredig boys shouted out, 'The bus is ready Nige, come on!' Out I went like a shot, but not quick enough to avoid the banter from the Tregaron boys! They were waving their fists in the air at me as the bus drove off!

DB I thought you were going to mention another story I remember you sharing, one involving the South Wales Police rugby team. That's a similar one, isn't it?

NO That was an ugly one! The same thing happened in that I went on Cefneithin's bus, the away team playing South Wales Police. The difference this time was that the Police team saw me arriving. Their response wasn't just banter. They gave me a really hard time throughout the game. I penalised them quite a few times in the match, correctly so of course, and then, after penalising them again in the second half, the captain led his players off the pitch saying they didn't want to play any more. That really shook me and my confidence. It made me question whether I wanted to carry on refereeing. I was only a 16-year-old schoolboy after all. Luckily enough Brian Phillips, who was in charge of the Police team, made sure that they came back on to finish the game. He looked out for me after the match too. If it wasn't for him that day, I probably would've packed it all in there and then.

DB Was that taken further then?

NO Yes it was, in that I had a visit a few days later from one of the Llanelli and District Referees' organisers, Onfel Pickard. He was a wonderful man. He came to the school and apologised for the Police team's behaviour and said it shouldn't have happened. He then told me in no uncertain terms that I shouldn't give up and that they would support me in every way they could.

DB That's interesting. Because, when I started there were a lot of complaints from the smaller clubs about the difference in standard between the ways they were reffed and the ways the bigger clubs were reffed. They felt that the big clubs, your Cardiffs, Neath and Llanelli, were allowed to get away with things that they weren't. That might have been true, but I can't see the bigger clubs walking off like that, either!

NO When you say bigger and smaller clubs, back then was that structure any different to today?

DB In terms of amateurism and professionalism, well things couldn't be more different of course. But, in another way, no there wasn't. You still had your grassroots, your middle

Cardiff player Jason Hewlett getting his marching orders from Derek

tier and the top flight, but they were organised differently to the way they are today. So the same but different, if you like. Organisationally, we both started in what I thought then was the best league in Wales, the West Wales League. I thought that's where the best rugby was played and it was the best organised too. It had 40 clubs at one time. But there was a step-up that I needed to take if I was to progress as a ref. I needed to move up to referee games between what you could call the second tier of rugby in Wales, your Abertillerys and Penarths. That was the next level for me, before I could referee Cardiff, Newport, Bridgend and the like. I was given an unexpected stepping stone to that level when I was asked to referee Neath versus Resolven at the Gnoll in a centenary match. I'd played on the Gnoll and, of course, I knew the pedigree of the Neath team. That match had Scottish international Wilson Lauder in the Neath team.

NO You didn't mention that to anyone though, did you Bev!

DB I might have mentioned it a few hundred times in the Vardre clubhouse Nige, and a few other clubhouses as well! I'd reffed my first international after all – player, if not match! After that game, in the 1978/79 season, I was moved up to the next level. I was now reffing Glamorgan Wanderers, Tredegar, Abertillery and the like on a regular basis.

NO How long was it before you took the next step up again, to level one?

DB That was only a year later. In 1979/80 I was reffing players such as the Pontypool front row, JPR Williams and Geoff Wheel. I was now in control of players that I had looked up to for many a year. I'll never forget the first time I reffed at Stradey Park. I must confess that I was a little overwhelmed. The match was Llanelli against Glamorgan Wanderers on a Tuesday night. It was given to me at the last minute so there wasn't much time to get my head around it. Some of the Vardre boys came with me as support, but that was at a personal cost to them as well. They had a bollocking for being there as they should have been in training!

In the tunnel, before walking out onto the pitch, I had a little bit of an emotional moment because I started to think about my late father and how I wished he could have seen me standing there, ready to go and referee the likes of Phil Bennett, Ray Gravell and JJ Williams. Even he, as a soccer man, would have been proud of me that day.

NO That's another one you kept quiet about, of course!

DB I couldn't wait to race back to Vardre and tell the boys that I had reffed such players and yes, I had even penalised them! Their response was quite something I must say. It went a little over and above the banter, and I could hear the phrase 'Bev reffed in Llanelli' spreading in hushed, respectful tones around the clubhouse. That was quite a feeling.

NO I suppose it was only a matter of time then before you had your first international.

DB I had to do a good three or four years of top-level club refereeing before I got my international chance. The system was different then. There was a two-tier international structure. Some internationals were recognised by the IRB and the players were given caps to play in them. Others were not recognised, and players didn't get caps even if they wore their country's shirt. An example of that is Gareth Jenkins, who played against Japan but didn't get a cap because Japan was not a member nation of the IRB. So, my international beginnings were on that lower level. I was sent abroad as well. That was a big change! In 1984 I reffed Italy versus Romania in L'Aquila to the east of Rome. I had a right royal welcome there too. The mayor came to meet me and I was driven in a limo to the ground. They were so pleased in that rugby-loving area to have been given the fixture – they more than pulled out all the stops! My two other unofficial Test matches were on Ireland's tour of Japan a year later.

You mentioned going on the Cefneithin team bus, and the furore that caused. Well, for that Ireland game in Japan, I flew out with the Irish team and sat next to their second row Wille Anderson. Once we were there, I ate meals with them and drank with them in the bar. I was even asked to go to some official functions with them! That led to them calling me Derek or Bev during the matches instead of the usual 'ref'. Hard to believe that now.

NO Can't say I've ever done that! I wouldn't be allowed to! Strangely enough, my first taste of international refereeing was also in Italy. But I don't remember having a civic reception or a limo! It was the Under-19 Rugby World Championships in 2002. My biggest game to date was during that tournament, South Africa versus New Zealand in the semi-final. That was held in Treviso. It went very well thankfully and the game itself was dominated by a certain youngster called Luke McAlister.

DB You were a fully-fledged WRU ref by then obviously, which meant that you had to venture further afield than just the west Wales district catchment area. How did you manage to get to the darkest valleys of the east by bus? That must have been an ordeal!

NO They were definitely the days of very long Saturdays! I would also referee a lot of Dewar Shield or school county matches on Saturday mornings and then go on to referee WRU matches in the afternoon. I'd leave early in the morning and not get back until late in the evening, all for an 80-minute game. But it had to be done. What about your Saturday pattern, Bev?

DB I would usually go to see my mother first as she lived nearby, but I would have put my kit out earlier in the morning. My boots would have been prepared way before that, on the previous Saturday night. I would wash my own kit, either on the Saturday night after a game or the Sunday morning. I think I only had to change my jersey once during a match. It was a really horrible day and Bridgend were playing Glasgow. Bridgend's jerseys were so dirty that they changed at half-time into their second strip of yellow. That then clashed with mine and I had to change to a green one. I'm glad I had a spare close at hand!

NO That's quite funny, because I had a very similar incident! When I started reffing I only had one jersey, a yellow one, or maybe it should be called a gold one because it was a replica Australian national team jersey I had bought at Owen Sports shop in Carmarthen. I progressed to having a second jersey which was a plain green one that my mum had sewn the Welsh Society of Rugby Union Referees' badge on to. I would then take the two with me to games. I turned up to referee a game between Betws Seconds and Nantgaredig Seconds. One team was in yellow, the other in green! I was stuck! Fair play, the Betws men came up with a quick answer. On the wall in their clubhouse was the framed shirt of one of their players who had won a Welsh

Under-19 cap. They took it out of the frame and gave it to me to wear during the game. That, of course, was a great opportunity for any supporter who wanted to have a go at me. And it happened. After one decision, penalising Betws for collapsing a scrum, one of their supporters shouted out, 'You may be wearing a prop's jersey, but you know f*** all about reffing them!'

There's no shortage of jerseys today, that's for sure. There are so many different ones for every different type of match. What were some early lessons that you learned then Bev, the ones that you experienced early on but they stayed with you throughout your career?

DB Right from the start I've always told myself that I should listen to advice. That can come from many different places. In Wales, of course, everyone is an expert on rugby and knows exactly how the game should be played. But you must choose who you take advice from. Usually, for me, it was from respected members of Vardre Rugby Club and some senior players. And other refs, of course. I remember one particular lesson that I learned as I was beginning to establish myself. I was given a Cup replay in Gorseinon. It was a difficult match. I knew one of the Gorseinon players, having played against him before. I ended up sending him off in that Cup replay and, to be honest, he was sent off because of bad refereeing. He was so frustrated by some of my calls and my arrogant attitude that he lost his temper. The custom is that the two teams clap the ref off the pitch at the end of the game. On that day they turned their backs on me. Supporters shouted at me, saying that they didn't want me there again and that the WRU could keep me. That was a tough lesson. I had thought that I was above that game and that I was too good for it. That attitude came out on the pitch. It never pays to have too high an opinion of yourself.

NO I took advice from many Pontyberem committeemen right from the start. I remember one man in particular who gave me very sound advice which helped me a lot – Eldon Lewis, the club secretary for years. He gave me one piece of advice I still remember. I was 17 when we had this conversation; I'd only just started reffing. I was in the Pontyberem clubhouse bar after a game. He came over to me for a chat. He said, quite simply, never referee a game with the whistle too close to your lips. He gave the example of Gwynne Walters, a former international ref. He usually wore a blazer when reffing and he kept the whistle in a blazer pocket. That meant that there was a delay between seeing an incident, reaching for the whistle, and then blowing it. That delay, Eldon said, gave him time to reflect and quite often he wouldn't blow his whistle as a result. Since then, I've held my whistle very low down to avoid the temptation of getting too whistle happy.

DB That was good advice. But you didn't buy a blazer though, did you?

NO Maybe not! I agree with what you said about listening to former players as well. That's particularly true of players in certain positions; usually they're in the scrum. When I was on the WRU referees' panel, Jon Humphreys came to talk to us, and then some time later I remember a one-to-one session with Robin McBryde when he tried to tell me what happens in the front row. I've learned a lot from Robin over the years, as well as from Paul Lloyd, a prop forward who played for Trimsaran and Pontyberem.

DB What I did early on was go and watch a lot of games when I wasn't reffing and then concentrate on particular aspects of play in those games. As an ex-flanker, I started to watch the back row play. But the front three remained a mystery for a long time after! The way I tried to understand what went on there was to sit in the bar with the props and hookers and talk about the game with them.

NO Did you learn anything?

DB No sooner than I would get the hang of it, the laws changed again!

NO Going back to the hard time you had in that Gorseinon Cup replay, how did you deal with the abuse thrown at you during or after a game?

DB People who say that criticism is like water off a duck's back to a ref are completely wrong. Of course name calling can hurt, just like it does with anyone else. Throughout my reffing career I've not met one ref who wasn't hurt by criticism at some time or another. What I was able to do, as the years went on, is learn how to deal with it. In the clubhouse after a match, for example, if people came up to me and said that such and such a decision was wrong, I would reply, 'You're absolutely right!' They didn't have a leg to stand on then!

NO But, of course, there are times when you might want to penalise someone, rightly or wrongly, when you first start out at least.

DB You're right, unfortunately. I remember one example of that in my experience that's particularly petty. I was at Stradey Park. My daughter had bought me a brand-new rugby shirt, a white one, for Christmas. I'd had the referee's badge sewn onto it. I was chuffed. You bought your own then, of course. I wore it with pride that day. Just before the match, I went into Cardiff's dressing room to inspect the players' studs. I approached Dai Joseph, their prop, who was in the process of greasing himself ready for the match. As I stood in front of him, he placed his hands on my shoulders so that he could lift one leg at a time and show me his studs. His grease-filled hands left two massive hand prints on my brand-new, clean, white shirt. It looked awful. I wasn't happy!

NO He'd upset the ref before he got on the pitch. Bad move!

DB Of course it was! First scrum, I penalised him for pulling the scrum down. He looked totally bemused, protesting his innocence. But it was three points to Bridgend. Next scrum, I penalised him again. He was even more bewildered, especially when the coach shouted from the side for him to sort his act out. Dai continued to protest his innocence and then he snapped, 'You're only doing this because I got your shirt dirty!' 'Too right I am!' I replied, and moved the game on. I'd made my point.

NO The other side of that, of course, is admitting when you actually have made a mistake and apologising for it. That's not easy, but it's essential if you are to gain long-term respect from players and officials alike, and even the fans as well. I did this once to none other than Martin Johnson. I was refereeing a Leicester game during his last season as a player. I'd made a wrong decision and I could see him storming over to talk to me, no doubt to tell me that I was wrong. But, before he opened his mouth, I told him, 'Sorry, I got that wrong.' He didn't know how to respond to that and just said, 'Ooh, humm, thank you!' The game carried on.

DB Absolutely. I've had to go after many a game and

apologise to players and coaches for getting something wrong. It's a painful thing to do. Every referee will make a mistake. That becomes a problem only when you make that same mistake again. Unfortunately, too many refs, even at the top level, try to make up for an obvious mistake by giving a penalty to the team they have wrongly penalised in a previous decision in order to restore the balance. All that does is show the ref to have made two mistakes. The more honest approach is to say, 'Alright lads, my fault. I'm sorry. Let's get on with it.' You'll have more respect if you do that than if you try to balance things out.

NO But, I seem to recall that you also taught me some ways to make you as the referee look a little better than you actually were when you got things wrong on the pitch.

DB I might well have done. We all make mistakes on the pitch, as we've said, but sometimes, now and again, you need to look after number one in such circumstances. On such occasions, when you know you've made the wrong call, the trick is to shout over to the assistant referee, 'Thank you! Thanks, so and so!' Everyone will then think that you acted on his advice and you look a little whiter than white. Can't say I did that often, but I did it quite a few times.

NO Of course there was a time when the touch judge wasn't allowed to intervene at all. That would have been the case when you started.

DB Absolutely! I remember my first game in charge as a ref when that new law came in. I was in, of all places, Pontypool Park, for a Welsh Cup quarter-final. The ground was packed. I'd never seen it so full and the atmosphere was fantastic. There was a line-out; Bob Norster won the ball for Cardiff and the play moved on. As I moved with it I could hear – and feel! – the crowd boo and shout in condemnation. I turned around to see Eddie Butler and John Scott, two international number 8s, eyeballing and scuffling with each other. I remembered that I was now able to call on my two touch judges to ask what had happened as I hadn't seen anything. On they came. One said that Butler had started the fight. The other said that Scott had thrown the first punch. They were both adamant they had seen everything, but they gave me two opposing accounts. What was I to do? In the end I turned to them both and said, 'Listen boys, we're in Pontypool Park. It's a Cup game. One player is a Welshman, the other is an Englishman. There are 16,000 people here. It's a penalty to Pontypool.' And that's how it was. I had a standing ovation from the home fans! As we walked off the pitch, John Scott turned to me and said, 'That was a good home decision wasn't it?' 'Too right it was,' I replied. As I said, no point denying the obvious.

NO What about the first time you were a touch judge, after they were allowed to intervene?

DB Funnily enough, that was a Cardiff game too. They were playing Newbridge and it was the semi-final after the quarter against Pontypool, which Cardiff obviously won. Clive Davis was in the second row for Newbridge. He had a few Welsh caps. He was up against Norster of course. In one line-out, after Norster had the best of Davis throughout the game, Davis decided to throw a punch at Norster's face. I saw it, clear as day. But Alan Richards, the ref, didn't see

Derek awards a try that delights Neath supporters during a Neath versus Cardiff Schweppes Cup game

Derek laying down the law to Kevin Moseley, and keeping a close eye on two of rugby's great scrum-halves, Rob Howley and Robert Jones

it. I thought to myself, well, Davis was lucky there. That was a clear sending off. He got away with it. A few minutes later I suddenly realised: Shit! I could have drawn the ref's attention to that! I had forgotten completely that I had new powers as a touch judge!

NO I think it's fair to say that neither of us relishes being touch judges. I certainly didn't at the start of my career. I've had to develop that part of my game in recent years, because the standard and responsibility has increased significantly. That's also taken a different twist recently. I've been put on the touchline for new young referees so that I can help and support them as much as I can in a match situation.

DB Oh, simple, I hated it. I liked to be the man in the middle, like you prefer to be. I used to spend a great deal of my time as touch judge talking to the supporters near me. Many a time I would be caught when the game had restarted after an injury or something, and I was still talking to some fans about the finer points of rugby!

NO What about the way coaches responded to you then Bev, especially after games? No doubt you had more than your fair share come up to you thinking they knew better than you, and players too no doubt.

DB Sometimes they actually did know better than me! I

remember coaches confronting me after a match, saying that I had failed to apply Law 22B sub-section C or whatever. I learned with time how to respond to that. I would say, 'Oh, OK, I'm sorry but I don't know that particular clause of the laws.' They would then say something like, 'Oh, so I know the laws better than you do?' 'On that particular point, yes you do. Well done!' And I would add, 'But I know it now, so look out next time I'll be reffing you!' That usually worked.

4

Tales of the First Games Together

With the career of one of these formidable referees up and running and the other just beginning, it was only a matter of time before they would officiate together. That happened in 1995. It was no ordinary occasion. It was Welsh legend Ieuan Evans' testimonial game. That in itself is significant. In terms of Welsh rugby, it was a game that looked back and forwards at the same time. It stands for how the game was changing, how it was moving on from the Bevan days to the days of Owens.

It was a rugby superstar event in the name of the then most capped Welsh player of all time. The big names of world rugby gathered at Stradey Park on 21 November 1995. Reiterating that fact at the start put paid to stories that the stars were only there because they were in the UK for Six Nations duty anyway. Such international weekends might well start days before the game, but not even the most ardent rugby fanatic starts his pilgrimage in November!

The Rugby World Cup had been held earlier that year and Derek Bevan officiated the semi-final. Ieuan Evans asked him to referee the testimonial. If the top ref was in place, the top players were as well: Sean Fitzpatrick, Jason Little, Thierry Lacroix, Olivier Roumat, John Gallagher, Rudolf Straeuli, the Hastings' brothers from Scotland, and many more. It was Ieuan Evans' British Isles XV versus an International Select XV. The biggest draw, in more ways than one, was the man mountain Jonah Lomu from New Zealand. The then 20 year old had taken the rugby world by storm, in a superstar kind of way. He was an explosive winger! He scored two tries at Stradey, as did the man of the moment and his opposite number, Ieuan Evans. His team beat the International Select XV 68–57, in a 19-try feast. The capacity crowd went home well fed!

The fact that such a game was given to Ieuan Evans speaks volumes of the respect his club had for him and for their continued enterprise in deciding how to honour him. The fact that so many stars came from far and wide to play in that game says so much about their regard for him. Over and above that, Ieuan reputedly pocketed £80,000 from the occasion. Yes, in the name of rugby. The game was changing. A football-type event to honour a star draws big names and earns the star big money.

Less than a year later, Llanelli's first star signing of the modern game would run out on that same turf. Frano Botica was enticed to Stradey by big money to mark a new era. More would quickly follow and, now of course, it's the norm.

Into such a game stepped the man with the whistle, the star ref Derek Bevan. On one of the flanks, the assistant referee, or touch judge in old money, was the up-and-coming star, Nigel Owens.

As it happens, there was a controversial incident in that game which involves the ref's assistants. Ieuan's team were losing 54–57 in the second half. They scored a try and Ieuan insisted he wanted to take the conversion. One of the Scottish players on the pitch that day, in writing about it in the *Scottish Herald*, says:

> In the second half Ieuan kicked the conversion which took us from 54–57 behind to a 61–57 lead (whether it actually went over or not is a private matter between Ieuan and the touch judges!).

Who knows, maybe two of the three officials that day, who are now involved with this book, might choose to reveal all for the very first time…

DB My assistants said it went over, so it must have!

NO I gave it on the day, so it must have been right!

DB It was quite a game that, and a joy to be part of it. I had known of Nigel beforehand of course. I had noted his rise up through the ranks, as it were. I remember I gave the last ten minutes to the other touch judge that day. I went off and he came on to referee. The Stradey faithful saw their chance. 'Game too fast for you is it, Bevan?' 'Can't keep up, can you?!'

Derek and Nigel at Ieuan Evans' testimonial game. Derek was referee, with Nigel and Mark Sayers as touch judges. Ken Parffit is in the middle.

NO I obviously knew about Derek Bevan before that game! This was the man who was in the World Cup semis just a few months before and who had reffed a World Cup final before that and I was to share a game with him. He was obviously someone any ref would more than look up to, at whatever stage of their career.

DB For my part, a few years before Ieuan's game, I had heard of this young 16 year old who had picked up the whistle while still at school. His early games were in the same west

Wales league as me of course. It wasn't that common to hear of a schoolboy showing an interest in reffing in those days, so I took a bit more notice to be honest.

That Ieuan Evans testimonial game was the beginning of a long association between Derek Bevan and Nigel Owens. It's one which continues to this very day and onto these very pages. As they were both active in their local referees' societies, they would soon begin to meet at referees' meetings. They would rarely meet on match days of course, as they both had their own respective games to officiate. They sometimes were touch judges for each other. There's one game to mention that brought the two of them together right at the end of Derek's career. In fact, it was his very last game before he retired. It was Nigel again who was in his least favoured role.

DB They asked me to referee the first game played under a closed roof at the Millennium Stadium. That happened to be my last game before retiring. It was a Welsh XV against the French Barbarians and Nigel was the touch judge for me that day. We had a bit of a party afterwards of course and, in the car on the way back, I confirmed that I was giving up. But it's appropriate again that, at my last game, you were there Nige.

NO It certainly was, looking back now. At the time, of course, I had no idea what was ahead of me. All I knew was that I had been able to work alongside one of the best refs in the world, and the best referee in the world for over a decade.

The link between the two strengthened significantly when Derek hung up his whistle in 2000. Derek's retirement created a gap on the WRU panel of first-class referees and that was duly filled by Nigel Owens. That's also when Derek became Nigel's refereeing coach.

DB In 2000 I thought that was the end of my involvement with the game. It was my good fortune that Nigel was up-and-coming and that I was asked to be a part of his career development. I'd been given an extension on my involvement with rugby. Coaching and TMO work extended it by twelve years. They were fantastic times. And, of course, since 1995 everything was professional. Throughout the 1995 World Cup we weren't paid. After that, it was £1,000 an international, and on from there. Prior to 1995 I had depended on the goodwill and support shown to me by my employers BP where I had worked for years. They were a great company to work for. In four World Cups, I had to have six weeks off each time. If it was the Tri-Nations, I was away for ten days or so at a time. I never lost a penny. Not only that, my workmates would cover for me, doing my shifts and helping however they could.

It was the way that rugby had been structured for decades before that. I was lucky. Towards the end of the 1990s, it was £500 for running touch. I couldn't believe it!

How fortunate I was that I worked for an employer like that. I can't imagine being a mechanic working in a garage and asking for six weeks off. It wouldn't have happened and my story would be completely different.

This new, professional era meant that Derek and Nigel worked together a great deal in an ever-changing game. This period provides a wealth of stories. You will read some of them over the next few pages. But first, Derek remembers having to respond to the fervent ambition of the young Nigel.

DB I think all referees are ambitious people, but Nigel was very, very ambitious. I remember a few occasions when I would suggest that Nigel should do something in a certain way, but he'd turn around to me and say, 'No, I'll do it this way.' My response would be, 'OK, carry on, but I bet you in a month's time you'll be back saying that you want to do it the way I originally suggested.' The truth of the matter was that I had tried to do things my own way when I started, and ended up listening to what more experienced refs told me. So I knew he'd come round to my way of thinking!

NO There's a saying in Welsh, Bev: *'Ysgol galed yw ysgol profiad'* 'The school of experience is a tough school.' That's what I went through at the time you're talking about. What are the first recollections you have of coaching me then, Bev?

DB Coaching was something that I really took to, I must say. It was a different way of keeping my involvement with the game. No one played that role in my development, so it was also good to have the chance to do something new. What it involved in practical terms was going with you to the games you officiated. Sometimes that meant going four or five Saturdays on the trot. Then it might be just once a month. This was to places like Pyle or Kenfig Hill. It wasn't first-class games we went to when I started with you. And, of course, when those first-class games came, as you worked your way up the ladder, I could watch you at every match of yours that was televised.

NO Do you remember any of those early ones?

DB Strangely enough, I do! It was one of the games I wasn't able to be at. I had a family do or something, and couldn't travel to Bath for the game you were reffing on the Rec. Luckily, it was on telly, and I watched it at home. During the game you were having a tough time with the forwards, and the front row in particular...

NO There's a pattern developing here!

DB Indeed! It got to the point in that Bath game that you had to have a word with the front three. You said, 'Gentlemen please, I'm asking you to stop this constant infringing. If it continues, someone's going to go, OK gentlemen?' You rang me after the game and told me that you had issues with the forwards. I told you that I already knew that as I'd seen the game on telly. And then I commented straightaway, 'What's all this nonsense with "Gentlemen" and "Please"? There are no gentlemen in the front row in the first place, and you don't say please as if you're asking them, you're f***ing telling them!'

NO I got the message alright, loud and clear!

DB To jump forward a bit, when I was TMO at some of your games you would refer back to that incident, indirectly at least.

NO You've got me there, Bev.

DB Well, I remember! If there was an incident involving the forwards, you would call them together to give them a telling off, and end your little speech with 'I've asked you, you're not listening; now I'm telling you!' Then you'd speak into your mic and say, 'What do you think about that then, Bev?' And I would sit there smiling, wanting to ask you back, 'Where did you get that phrase from then, Nige?' But it showed you'd learnt!

NO I remember it well! Bristol against Leinster in the

Heineken Cup. My first real big game in that competition. I couldn't get away with that now because there's so much more scrutiny as to what we can and can't say to the TMO. And so many more people listening in! We spent hours together regularly in that period, talking about what you could call the little things. It was amazing for me to talk about really key issues such as the way you talk to players, the need for honesty, accuracy, and when it was right to make a quip and when it was not. And you were happy to make your views on refereeing standards public as well when you were asked to contribute to any rugby broadcast.

DB I'm not sure which game you're referring to Nige, but there's one I remember. I was commentating for the BBC on a game between the Dragons and Ulster. The ref was particularly bad that day. There was a fight on the pitch and he grinned and smiled at those involved as he dealt with them. I had to comment on air. 'If there's any young referee watching,' I said, 'that's exactly how *not* to deal with an incident like this. If you've taken a punch and then you look up afterwards to see the ref smiling and grinning, all that's going to do is make you want to take revenge in some way or other.' The same ref, a Scottish one, was involved in another incident during a game between the Dragons and Scarlets.

NO The story with Scott Quinnell?

DB Exactly! He was taken off the ball and then went looking for retaliation. That was shown in the form of a not-so-subtle forearm tackle which took the other guy right out. The Dragons crowd went berserk! They called him an unclean person of dubious parentage! Former Welsh international Tony Clement was sitting next to me in the commentary box. He asked me on air, 'What do you think, Derek?' 'Oh, he's gone,' was my instant reply. There were no replay screens in those days, but there was no need for any in this instance. It was a straightforward sending off offence. Next thing, the ref pulls out a card – but it was a yellow! Scott's face was a picture. He couldn't believe it himself. I've never seen a man more thrilled to get a yellow card!

NO I remember that very clearly because you went through it with me afterwards as an example of how not to do things. You told me that it was a classic illustration of a ref looking at the face and not at the incident. Scott, the British Lion, is what he saw, and you said that if it had been anyone else it would have been a red. Having said that, we've all probably done something similar at some point or other.

DB I remember your first big game too on the international stage. It was a B international, and once again it was back in Bath, funnily enough. It was the English Saxons against their French counterparts.

NO I don't mind you remembering that one at all! That's a match that went very well for me and I was as high as a kite after it. What a feeling. That was the biggest event I had been in charge of up to that point and it was a big step up. But it wasn't only the on-field things you would coach me on, was it? It was more to do with the bigger picture of being a referee. I remember you telling me about a game when Bob Yemen, the referees' manager, was there watching. You both left the game in the same car, and Bob started to go on about the expenses you were submitting. Your response was to turn the radio up so loud that you couldn't hear him talking. Then the radio jumped to Radio Cymru, which neither of you could understand, but you left it on until he stopped talking about expenses! He never brought the subject up again with you!

DB Of course! There's so much more to being a ref than the 80 minutes or so on the pitch. One of the early things I passed on to you, if you remember, was what to do after the game ended.

NO I certainly do! You encouraged me to spend some time after every game in the clubhouse with the players and officials of both teams. Even if it's only for ten minutes, you told me, it's important to give people the opportunity to talk to you. But I wasn't to impose myself in any way, just to make myself available.

DB That's right. Half-past four on a Saturday afternoon might well not be the best time to talk things through with coaches, especially if things haven't gone too well for them that day. One thing that's so true in the game of rugby, and many other sports as well no doubt, is that if things aren't going well for you as a club, you look for someone to blame. More often than not, that person is the ref. You always have to keep that in mind. But it doesn't mean you don't deal with everyone in the same way after the game. If a coach wants to talk to you, he'll come to you. He'll find you.

NO That struck me at the time. You weren't telling me to go looking for the response from any coach, in the sense of actually asking them, 'How did I do today then?' That wasn't the thing to do.

DB Certainly not! If you said that, as too many young referees today tend to do, you really are opening yourself up for an answer you might not like at all! They really will f***ing tell you. If a coach wants to talk to you, he'll come to you. But you've got to be there for him to do so, and it's worth going to the clubhouse, having a glass of shandy or whatever, and being seen to be a part of the event.

NO That was your approach on the pitch itself as well, wasn't it, at the end of a game?

DB Same principle exactly. Don't rush up to players after the final whistle, from whichever team. It's far more professional to wait on the pitch, removed from both teams, but always close at hand if they choose to approach you, which more often than not they do.

NO In addition to that I remember you impressing on me how important it was not only to deal with others – the officials and players – in a proper manner, but also to look after myself. I remember you telling me that if I'm not going to like the answer, don't ask the question.

DB Quite right. And I remember an incident with you where I first noticed the need for impressing that point on you. It was an international Sevens tournament and you reffed New Zealand against Samoa. One of the Samoans laid out an All Black, a straightforward red card. You walked over to the touch judge and asked him for his opinion. Following your chat, you gave the red card. I remember asking you after that, 'Did you see the incident?' 'Yes,' you said. 'Did you think it was a red card offence?' 'Yes,' you said. 'So in that case, why did you ask the touch judge's opinion? He's the one being seen to show all the bravery and courage of his conviction and you've been shown to lose a little bit of respect. Everyone is now saying "fair play to the touch judge" when you could have been having that acclaim instead of him. The publicity would have been: "No-nonsense referee Nigel Owens sends man off." But the story ended up actually saying that the referee, after consultation with his touch judge, made the call. It's not the same. And you'd seen the incident as it was and called it right in the first place!' Basically, you were missing opportunities to impress.

NO I remember you saying, after the match, that I had given people an opportunity to criticise me. I needed, you said, to be more selfish in one sense, and think about my own career and profile. If I was sure of the decision, you said, I should make it myself. That was a valuable lesson.

DB No doubt. As you're climbing up the ladder, that little bit of self-doubt creeps in and starts to take over. I get that. It's a lack of confidence. But there were other times when you showed tremendous confidence.

NO Am I going to like this bit?

DB I don't know. But it happened. I'm referring to a time when you came to me to tell me you'd had your assignments for the first round of that season's European fixtures. And you weren't very happy to say the least. You had a game in Europe in the second tier but you didn't have a European Cup game. 'And the problem is?' I asked you. To which the reply was that you thought you were being mollycoddled.

NO And if I remember correctly, you had quite a direct response!

DB I did. 'Yes, you are being mollycoddled,' I said, 'because you're not ready yet!' I also had the assignments for the second round of European fixtures in front of me when you told me that, and I could see that you also only had the second-tier fixtures then too.

NO And my response to that was to say, yes, I was ready but how could I prove that if I wasn't given the opportunity to do so?

DB Sometimes, I said, you've got to bite the bullet and just take your time patiently. You weren't the only one who wanted those kinds of opportunities. You didn't like me saying that at the time. But, your talent aside, other factors happened to kick-in at that point to move your career forward.

NO Indeed. They involved other referees' fortunes. One retired and the other was going through a bad patch. So, all of a sudden, I was in favour probably sooner than I would have been otherwise. The European Cup games came sooner than I expected. All of a sudden it was fixtures such as Wasps against Toulouse. It was quite a change. The first big test for me was Leinster against Munster. What a game and what an experience. It was quite a change from the fixtures I was usually getting.

DB That, of course, meant far more foreign travel...

NO Don't tell me, this is where the story of my first trip abroad happens, told of course completely impartially by you!

DB It would be so wrong not to mention it, Nige! I was asked to go with you for your first European game abroad, just to look after you, as it were! We got to the airport and you wanted to do things properly and write an address on the label of your suitcase. So you asked me for the name of the hotel we were staying at. I replied, 'Number 1, High Street, Treviso.' And you dutifully wrote that down on the label!

NO All of you just creased with laughter at me being so naïve! I had the radio communication equipment with me as well, didn't I? We had to carry the comms ourselves in those days. But your leg-pulling didn't stop there, did it?

DB Of course it didn't! As we were walking out to the plane, you asked the rest of us which one was ours. We pointed to one on the runway and said, 'That's it Nige, you go first!' Off you went towards the wrong plane as we went towards

Nigel getting wired up with the communication system before a Tri-Nations match in Hamilton, New Zealand.

the right one. We called you back just in time, before you could be questioned by airline staff, which would have been fun as you were carrying a case full of radio equipment as well!

As the two spent more and more time together, they got to know each other really well, and conversations would be about so much more than just rugby. One common topic was the background and upbringing they both shared – the mining communities of south Wales.

DB You were always interested Nige in the fact that I had been working underground. No doubt that was because your father had, as had so many other relatives and neighbours. We shared a lot about what it was like to be brought up in such communities. In one way Clydach and Pontyberem are very different places. But coal links them both and gives them something in common that is very strong. We both shared that.

NO I remember one story. We were on a train to some match or other, four of us. We were playing cards and talking about just that. The chat then moved on to how we all got involved in refereeing. You said that you had an accident and I asked you what it was like on the coalface.

DB We were in the Chunnel, on our way to Paris. I said how bad the conditions were. Men could hardly walk; they had to carry asthma pumps around with them all the time because breathing was difficult. I said that Margaret Thatcher and Arthur Scargill had a hard time for closing the mines between them, and that was a massive blow to areas like ours, no doubt. But, on the other hand, it was a blessing of sorts that men didn't have to work in such conditions any more. They're best closed.

NO I was surprised to hear you put it like that, but I really understood why you said it. We spoke then about what you did underground, didn't we?

DB I was an electrician, as I've said, and one of my responsibilities was testing for gas using the old Davy lamps. In the old days, I said, they used canaries to test for gas. When someone asked how that was done, I said that the canaries were kept in a cage in the manager's office. If there was a need to test for gas, either because we didn't know if there was any in a particular section of the coalface, or because we thought there might be, then the canary would be sent in a cage on the end of a long stick into the area in question. If there was gas the canary would die, and the men knew not to go into that area until the gas was dealt with. You were intrigued by that Nige, and asked me, 'Did the canaries die very often?' To which I replied, 'No, only once!' Well, the others were in their doubles laughing, as well as some of the passengers around us in the train who had heard what I said.

NO You liked to make me look a bit simple, didn't you!

DB Couldn't do it now though, Nige!

Derek Bevan coached Nigel Owens for the best part of six years. He followed him through every stage of his development, through every competition and to nearly every rugby-playing nation. When that coaching came to an end, it certainly wasn't the end of their friendship, nor was it the end of their working relationship. Three new letters had entered the rugby vocabulary by then, TMO, the Television Match Official. The man – and they always are men – who sits in a small booth watching the televising of the game so that he can check any incident the ref asks him to through the use of multiple camera angles and slow motion. Derek has been Nigel's TMO dozens and dozens of times over many years.

DB Early on in our ref-TMO relationship, we developed a code between the two of us. If Nigel and his two assistant refs missed something, like an obvious forward pass or an off-side, I would whisper this codeword through my mic into Nigel's earpiece and Nigel would know that something needed to be checked. The codeword was Trigger – straight out of *Only Fools and Horses*! But, Nigel's own TV involvement put a stop to that.

NO It certainly did. I was on the set of the *Jonathan* series I do with Jonathan Davies for S4C. I happened to mention to Jiffy that we had this Trigger system going between me and Bev. That was the end of that, I thought. Not long afterwards, with Jiffy doing his match commentating role live on air, an incident occurred in the game. I wasn't reffing in that one. I think it actually was a forward pass, missed by the ref. Jiffy told the whole watching public, 'Of course, that wouldn't happen between Nigel and Derek because they've got codes.'

I'll never forget a game in France between Clermont and Leinster. You were in the TMO truck and news came through that Trigger from *Only Fools and Horses* had died. During a stoppage in play, you said to me, 'Nige, Trigger is dead. It will have to be Rodney now if you miss something!' I started giggling to myself on the pitch and the two front rows were looking at me, shaking their heads in bewilderment.

DB Of course we weren't allowed to have codes! A TMO official in Dublin came to hear about this and we were told that we had to stop. Well, we *sort* of stopped. We replaced 'Trigger' with Welsh words. No one, certainly in England, France and any other country abroad, knew what was being said.

NO At that time the TMO was only allowed to answer questions asked of him by the ref. Ironically, that has changed now and they are allowed to intervene to draw the ref's attention to something he might have missed. Bev and I did that anyway – we started it! We've certainly moved on now from the days you mentioned when a new development was allowing touch judges to indicate foul play for the first time!

DB It's a lot more complicated than that now, for certain. And, as you said earlier on that touch judge issue, you've had to sharpen that part of your game significantly because of the way rugby has gone in recent years. I think that's only fair. When you or I would referee a match, we would want 100 per cent from our touch officials. So why wouldn't we give 100 per cent to a ref when we were running touch? I didn't always see it that way, I must be honest.

5

Tales on the Road

In the rugby world the Welsh have always had a reputation for being very good at socialising. That was a factor on the successful Lions tour of 1971, for example. Tales were told of how players from the other three countries were amazed that the Welsh were always invited for Sunday lunch and so on in the homes of exile Welsh families who had settled in New Zealand. It would appear that this tradition is true of Welsh referees as well. No doubt this causes the same bemusement to officials from other countries as much as it does to their player counterparts.

Derek and Nigel spend a great deal of time together on the road and a good deal of that time seems to revolve around socialising, which inevitably leads to some fine tales. Here's a handful of them, beginning with the game when Derek upset Roger Quittenton with his lack of pre-match instruction: the one where he said, 'Same as last week boys!' That was a match at London Irish.

DB They were always known for being good with their after-match hospitality, and this game was no exception. In fact, it was one of the best.

NO They had a live band on stage that night too. It was brilliant.

DB All of a sudden, they asked me and you and one of the other officials with us to go up on stage to sing. So there we were, singing Tom Jones songs. I remember singing 'It's Not Unusual' at least, can't remember what else. And then Nigel did his usual star turn, which means he sang that old Welsh love song, 'Myfanwy'. Oh my gosh, it went down so well. It silenced a room full of rowdy rugby fans!

NO It was an amazing response, I must say. I'm quite used to singing that at rugby functions but that was one of the special ones. I think the London Irish fans have always appreciated my singing more than my refereeing!

DB But it's not only at rugby functions you sang that song, is it? Do you remember Paris? We might have been there in the name of rugby, but this performance had nothing to do with the match!

NO I do remember, yes, and you had a part to play in what happened – again! We were in a restaurant enjoying some downtime and a good meal before flying home after refereeing a match at Racing Metro. At the same venue there was a party going on for an old lady who was celebrating her eightieth birthday. Some of the family recognised me and Derek and came to ask for photos. Derek started talking to one of them and asked him, when I was distracted with the photography, did he know that I sang as well? The Frenchman didn't. They then asked me if I would be so kind as to sing a song in Welsh for the old lady. How could I say no! It was impossible to refuse on such a happy occasion. So up I went and sang 'Myfanwy' at a birthday party in the middle of Paris!

DB The old lady was so, so happy and Nige was star of the show!

NO Over the years I've sang quite a bit at this restaurant. I went there with various match officials during the 2007 World Cup. So I knew the owner, Maurice, and his family quite well by the time of the old lady's party. I also knew that the restaurant had a particular custom. After the entertainment, Maurice would push out a trolley of Armagnac. The waiter would then go around asking everyone for their year of birth and serve them with an Armagnac from that year. He asked me and I said 1971. The other officials, Nigel Whitehouse and Hugh Watkins, gave their dates of birth. I'm not sure you'd seen this before Bev, but if you hadn't you cottoned on to it pretty quickly. Do you remember what you said when they asked you what year you were born?

DB 1951 and 1953!

NO We were rolling with laughter! Needless to say they didn't fall for it, and you only had one brandy like everyone else. But at least they made it a large one for you!

DB Fair play to them! There was another story involving brandy before a game in France, wasn't there?

NO The semi-finals of the European Cup, Toulouse against Leinster…

DB No way! It wasn't a Euro semi was it? I don't remember that bit!

NO Well it was. I think it was some sort of celebration. It could have been my fiftieth game or something similar. I was ref and you were TMO and there was one Welsh and one English assistant ref and there were two Welshmen as refs numbers four and five.

DB Bloody hell, you've got a good memory!

NO My routine the night before a game is quite simple really. I'll have a meal with the other officials at which I'll have a half or a full glass of wine and that's it. Most of the time it's just Diet Coke. I think you're the same Bev, aren't you?

DB Yes indeed. Certainly, when I'm reffing. It might be different if I'm TMO, which I was at that game and that's a relevant part of the story isn't it?

NO It is. You like your brandy, as we've already said. So this particular evening you might have had two doubles because it was a celebration. Anyway, during the game itself the day after there was a kick at goal, either a penalty or a conversion. At this stadium the lights are on the roof of the stand, and they can make life difficult for some decisions if the ball is high up in the air. When this kick went high above the posts, the two officials didn't raise their flags or keep them down. They didn't know if the ball was over or not. So I had to ask you to decide. It was replayed and replayed on screen as usual and, during this process, Hugh Watkins, who was with us the night before, says into his radio, 'I bet you're sorry you had those brandies last night now, Bev!'

DB I think that was a cover-up for the fact they didn't know what had happened! Blaming the lights and then the quip at me!

As we've already seen, Derek and Nigel have been involved with many a rugby milestone over the years. One such occasion was the first club rugby union game to be played at the mecca of Gaelic football, Croke Park. The first ever rugby union game played there was Ireland against France in the Six Nations in 2007. Derek and

Nigel were there for that first club game, the Heineken Cup semi-final, an all-Irish encounter between Munster and Leinster. Up until that point, Munster were the dominant Irish rugby force in Europe, having been champions twice, including the previous season. So they were defending champions. But Leinster won that semi. It was the turning point of their European fortunes. They were European champions that season and they have been three times since as well. At the time, that game in 2009 held the world record attendance for a rugby club match.

NO It was one of the greatest club matches I have been involved in. In fact, I think it was the greatest. It was also the game that Alan Quinlan, the Munster and Irish forward, was cited for gouging Leo Cullen's eyes. Unfortunately for him, it cost him a place on the Lions tour that year. That was a real shame as he was a fantastic player who deserved his place on that Lions trip. One moment of madness took that away from him. But that was the only remote shadow over the occasion. It was a fantastic day.

DB Oh, it was marvellous! The streets of Dublin were packed with supporters, flags, banners and music. The atmosphere was superb. It was better than an international day, and that's saying something! On top of that, it was a very good game of rugby as well. Munster were favourites, but Leinster beat them comprehensively, 25–6.

NO We'd got a great flavour of that atmosphere the day before. It's the best atmosphere I've experienced, I must say. Quite something. Everyone was in good spirits with plenty of banter. So, that night we went out for our usual meal as officials. Halfway through we hear the people on the table next door singing 'Happy Birthday'. As they are finishing, a waitress gives the one having the birthday a whisky. When she came to ask what we wanted for dessert, you told her, 'Excuse me! It's my birthday today as well.' I knew that that wasn't the case as your birthday is in September and this was May!

DB Fair play, she responded politely and said, 'No problem, I'll be back now.' Great, I thought. Back out she comes. Everybody starts to sing 'Happy Birthday' to me and she presents me with... a fairy cake with a candle on it! I was gutted!

NO That definitely was our time to laugh at you, Bev. And we certainly did. Your face said it all – expecting a whisky and you get a fairy cake! Serves you right.

DB OK, fair enough! But it's interesting isn't it, to go back to rugby now, how things can be so different if only one small thing went in a different direction. Leinster were in that game because they had beaten Harlequins the week before in the quarter-finals. You were ref Nige, and I was TMO.

NO That famous game now referred to as 'Bloodgate'. What a match!

DB Yes it was, but unfortunately not because of the rugby that was played. It's one of the stains on the game in recent years, that one.

The match they refer to was the Heineken Cup quarter-final between Harlequins and Leinster at the Quins' home ground, the Stoop. It was played on 12 April 2009. It wasn't a free-flowing game. Towards the end of the second half the score was 6–5 to Leinster; Mike Brown scoring a try for the home team and Argentinian star Felipe Contepomi kicking two penalties for the Irish team. And then the drama unfolded. The Quins had lost their goal-kicking machine, Nick Evans, to injury. His replacement, Chris Malone, had missed the conversion of Brown's try. One kick could win it for the Quins. So they indicated to the ref, Nigel Owens, that wing Tom Williams needed treatment for a cut lip. He went off, and the previously injured Evans took to the field again, being allowed to do so because he was replacing an injured player. But Williams did not have a cut lip at all. He had been instructed to bite into a blood capsule to fake an injury so that Evans could come back on. He was caught on camera winking at someone as he walked off. This was the first indication that there was more to what had happened. The TV commentator, in fact, suggested that maybe Tom Williams had hit himself deliberately. But, in the pace and drama of a European quarter-final, there was no immediate indication that there was anything wrong, and the match continued. Leinster held on to their one-point lead.

NO I had no idea at all that any trick or cheating had taken place. It was impossible for me to know that without being medically trained and able to carry out medical checks there and then. All I could do was make sure that the player coming on for him was substituted and not replaced. Only a subbed player can come on for blood, and not one replaced through injury. I checked with those I should have checked with, and correctly allowed Nick Evans back on. When it dawned on me, after the game, what was being suggested happened, I naturally questioned myself a lot, asking if I should have seen what had happened? I went over the whole injury replacement incident, Williams going off, Evans coming on, time and time again. I regretted, without doubt, that I hadn't checked Williams' injury more rigorously. One thing that played back in my mind continuously is that I saw Evans warming up on the touchline a few minutes before Williams' injury. When the injury was called, I asked the physio if Williams was bleeding and he said, 'Yes he is, there's a cut in his mouth.' I looked at his mouth and saw the blood. After the event I thought a lot that maybe I should have asked him to wash his mouth out so that I could see the cut. But, even then, if I would have been told by the medical guy that the cut was behind his teeth, I would have had to take his word for it because I'm not medically trained. If I had seen the wink Tom Williams gave the dugout as he left the field, I might have been a bit more suspicious. But, to be honest, you don't really expect this kind of thing to happen in a match you're involved in. It was a very complex situation to unravel. In fact, it took four months for the investigation to uncover what had actually happened. The saving grace for the game was that it didn't affect the result. That would have been an even bigger mess to sort out.

DB And for me, as TMO, there was nothing obvious to see. There wouldn't be, of course. The investigation you mention showed that the Quins had done the same thing, with the blood capsules, on four previous occasions. And I'm sure that other teams have done the same as well. The Quins were lucky not to get thrown out of the European competition altogether after that. But the authorities decided that the punishments that followed were sufficient. Dean Richards, Quins' Director of Rugby, was banned for three years and other club officials were either banned or resigned. Tom Williams, the winger, was banned from playing for twelve months and the club was fined something like a quarter of a million pounds.

NO But it did lead, as well, to an agreement within the English Premiership that opposition doctors are allowed to examine players if they have any suspicions about injuries. And that was a good move.

The 'Bloodgate' scandal. Nigel trying to get some order on the touchline, with Derek keeping a close eye on his TMO monitors.

(Photo: David Rogers, Getty Images)

DB When you think of that marvellous occasion in the Croke Park semi-final, how different things could have been if the quarters a few weeks before had taken a different turn. When Evans came back on he attempted a drop goal which, if it had gone over, would probably have given Quins the victory and they would have been in the semis.

NO Can you imagine it if Harlequins had won, and won the whole European tournament even, and then the scandal of the blood capsules was made known? What would the European rugby authorities have done about that then, I wonder? Thankfully, for the good of rugby, it didn't come to that.

119

DB And it meant that we had that fantastic semi-final at Croke Park! It turned out alright in the end.

Some of these 'on the road stories' show us some particular characteristics of Nigel Owens' approach to the game. At the Paris party his popularity, away from home, is shown clearly by the guests' response to him. His subsequent singing shows a talent he had way before he picked up the whistle. He has always been an entertainer. But the more personal side of Nigel's life has also been the subject of public scrutiny, and, on occasions, influenced his game. Again, Derek Bevan has first-hand experience of this.

DB I remember a game between Northampton and Perpignan when the French side were in the top tier of French rugby. The Northampton prop, Brian Mujati, hit you Nige from behind and floored you. I was TMO but at that time we weren't allowed to talk to the ref without being asked. So it was a tricky one. Did he do it deliberately? I thought he did. He tried to make it look accidental, but his aim was to have a go at you Nige, without a doubt.

NO It was tricky. I didn't see anything of course because it was behind me. I knew well enough that I had been shoved and that I wasn't in the way because I was standing away from the line of entry into the ruck. Because he was a big prop I, for sure, felt the impact. But I had no idea what the motive was for the hit. I had a word with him as soon as play broke down after the incident, and asked him to be careful. I told him, 'You push me in the back again like that and you'll be off!' To which the match commentator responded, 'If he pushed you in the back, he should be off anyway.' The problem was I didn't see what exactly happened. I might have felt it, but that wasn't enough. So a warning was all that I could give under the circumstances.

But it's true to say that it was a very difficult game for me generally. Things were going against Northampton all through the match and I found it particularly tough to be in the middle of it all. They were well behind at the time of Mujati's push anyway. The disgruntled fans no doubt just saw my lecturing Mujati as one more thing that was going against them. It comes back to what you said earlier Bev, that a team facing difficulties needs a scapegoat and it's usually us. It was made worse, of course, by the fact that they lost the game in the end as well.

DB I think Mujati was cited for that, wasn't he? And then he was banned for six weeks after his disciplinary hearing in Dublin. Thank goodness that citing had been introduced by then. That was very unprofessional play.

NO But the problem for us was that we had flown down to Perpignan on the same plane as loads of Northampton fans and the team. Which meant, of course, that we had to fly back with them.

DB That's when it got nasty, I must say. We were at the airport, in the departure lounge. It was full of Northampton fans. We knew that we would get stick, Nigel in particular, and I warned him that would be the case. And, sure enough, the banter started. That wasn't too bad. It's more than normal in rugby of course, and you either blank it out or appreciate the cleverer, wittier comments. But one guy decided that he wanted to make sure that everyone knew what he thought of Nigel and that he wanted Nigel to know as well.

NO He stood close to us, close enough for him to know that I could hear everything he said. The usual comments came out about referee bias and incompetence and wrong decisions. But then he started to get really personal, making comments about my sexuality which crossed the line completely.

DB I was fuming sitting next to you! That man made me really angry and I knew that he had hurt you. I turned to one of the other officials sat next to me and said, 'If that guy goes to the toilet, I'll go in after him and flatten him!' It didn't come to that luckily. But the harm was done to Nigel.

NO It was a very long flight back, I can tell you. But, thankfully, the majority of the fans were good, decent rugby supporters. They certainly didn't like the fact that they had lost and they didn't agree with some of my decisions. But they accepted that they were beaten by a better team and the chat between us was very respectful.

DB You closed your eyes and tried to ignore the banter that continued on the plane. But, no doubt, you didn't sleep a wink because of what was said in that departure lounge.

NO I hadn't experienced that kind of personal insult before and it did hurt, there's no doubt about that. It had nothing to do with the way I reffed the game. If I did make mistakes, which I did, it wasn't because I am gay. There was no need for it at all. That particular fan was disciplined by the club and well done them for doing so.

DB There's no use pretending that comments don't hurt. They do affect your game at times. You went through a rough patch not long after that, didn't you?

NO Coming out of the World Cup in 2007, I was pretty much on top of my game. But then, all of a sudden, for about ten or eleven months before the 2011 World Cup, things started to go downhill. There were the Autumn Internationals, a couple of European games and Scotland Ireland in the Six Nations. I didn't referee the Scotland Ireland game well at all. I can't put my finger on why. I don't think it was the homophobic abuse I'd had at Perpignan airport. I was in a difficult relationship at the time. I'm sure that was the main reason for it.

DB Do you think it had something to do with missing your mum?

NO She passed away not long before the bad patch I hit, so that could well have been the reason, or one of the reasons. We were very close and maybe that played on my mind more than I thought after she passed away. It's possible that feeling her loss affected the way I responded to situations and decisions.

DB I think it was that, personally. I think it hit you hard. It might well not have been helped by some other factors, no doubt. In our conversations you started to make comments that were out of character. You were asking questions that weren't you. I remember one clear example. You were thinking of dropping out of one international game altogether because of how you felt. I had not heard that from you before. We talked about it quite a lot at the time and thought through all the options. In the end I said to you, after much thought, 'Take the game Nige, and do it for one person. Do it for Mam.'

NO And I did, thankfully. That helped me no end personally and it was also a significant part of me building up my game again in readiness for the World Cup ahead. Paddy O'Brien, who was in charge of us refs at the time, told me in no uncertain terms when I was in the middle of that darker period that I might well still be able to go to the World Cup, but that I wouldn't be there as a leading official unless I bucked up my ideas. Things did turn around, luckily, and I went to the 2011 World Cup in a stronger position than I was when Paddy spoke to me.

DB The Northampton incident you just mentioned was the first time you had homophobic slurs aimed at you, but it wasn't the last time was it? Twickenham happened in 2014. I wasn't with you then, but we talked about what you were going through. That was when two England fans shouted homophobic comments at you from the crowd at Twickenham.

NO Again, the abuse was uncalled for and unnecessary. But what was good about that whole story was the way it was dealt with. The RFU were quick to deal with it and they sent out a clear message that such abuse, homophobic or otherwise, was not to be tolerated in the sport. I welcomed that response and their action in banning the two men who shouted the comments for two years from Twickenham.

DB And they were ordered to pay £1,000 each to a charity of your choice, weren't they? That was good action by the RFU, certainly.

NO I remember my comments at the time. On Radio 5 Live I think it was. In referring to the men charged with the verbal abuse, I suggested in the first place that I meet with them in order for them to explain why they said what they said. I then said on the programme that I'd tell the two men to think twice about saying the things they'd said to me, because it's actually not me they're hurting, it's the young kid sitting in the row in front who's maybe dealing with his or her own sexuality. The most difficult thing I ever had to do in my life was accept that I was gay. It's someone sitting two seats away, going through what I went through, dealing with who they are; they are the people they're putting in danger.

Nothing excuses what the two men at Twickenham or the one Northampton fan said in Perpignan. But, looking back at the two incidents and the comments from the three men, I'm heartened by the way that the game of rugby as a whole, across the world, has responded to those incidents. The support, the unquestioning backing I've had, has been amazing!

6

A Few Thoughts
From Them Both

These pages have shown clearly how Derek and Nigel have seen many changes in the world of rugby over the decades. They started refereeing in completely different eras. You could almost think that it wasn't the same game at times. But how do they see the game now from those different perspectives? That's what follows here, as they bring to an end their insightful and entertaining conversation on what it's been like to be the top men in the middle of a rugby pitch.

DB When I think of the game today, I can tell you one thing – I would so miss being able to say some of the things to players that I could get away with saying then, but you can't now Nige! It was easy for me to whisper in the ear of a forward, usually, and tell him exactly what I thought of him, in my best French. There's no such thing as a quiet word now!

NO No, it's full scrutiny all round now. You can't breathe without someone hearing you. It took me a while to get used to the electronic equipment when it was first introduced. It was strange being on the pitch and hearing the comments of the officials on the touchlines. And, they made those comments by speaking into the flags they were carrying! It's a little more sophisticated now, with all officials linked up to one another. And, of course, in televised games the ref's mic is available to all the people sitting and watching at home as well. We carry around, on average, about 3kg when we are wearing all the gear. That includes the ref cam. I'm used to that now, but it was a definite technological adjustment for a while. You soon fall into the routine though, and it wasn't too difficult to remember not to speak out of turn. It's certainly a challenge for those of us who are prone to swearing from time to time.

DB More microphones certainly, but far more cameras at games now too, and more officials. Today there are six officials at any one game. When I was refereeing it was just one. The ref. That's it! That's why I say it's easier to referee these days than it was then. There was literally no hiding place. The buck stopped with you and no one else. But, for some reason, refs today don't seem to like me saying that and disagree with me. Can't think why!

NO You would say that, wouldn't you Bev? But I don't think you're right! Well, not completely anyway. In one way you are. It was all down to you in those days, and therefore there was nowhere to hide. You didn't even have neutral touch judges to rely on. They were invariably from the two teams on the pitch and would have been completely biased!

But, in another way though Derek, it's a lot harder today, even though there are more of us. The game has changed. It's a much faster game; the ball is in play a lot more. You can't referee it as it is on your own any more. But, more than that, technology plays a massive part. Before, you wouldn't know what the fans in Glasgow, Leicester or Limerick thought about any game. All the chatter would be within the four walls of local pubs. Now I can find out what fans all over the world think before I'm back in my car at the end of a game. That's a pressure which makes many referees and players stay off social media. On the pitch, obviously, as we've touched upon already, every frame of every move is analysed, resulting in the refs having to be forensic in their decisions. You might well not have known of any mistakes you would have made, especially if the game wasn't televised. Maybe you made even more than you thought!

DB You make a good case, Nige! One direct thing that's come from both the increase in officials and cameras at matches is that I don't think there's such a thing as the blind side any more, not from a ref's point of view anyway. Maybe there is if you're a player, and technically there is that side that's the 'other side'. But in no way is it blind in that you can't see what happens there. Every angle is covered. That's changed the game.

NO What do you make of the TMO coming into the game more now than ever before then, Bev? I know you go along with it because you were one for years. But what do you think that's done to the game?

DB In one way it's made refereeing easier, but in another way it hasn't made it easier at all. I've seen many a referee not make a decision he would otherwise have made because he knows the TMO can make it for him. For example, they won't make an attempt to say if a try has been scored or not because the camera can show that. Some referees don't even try to get into the correct position in order to see what's happened in play and then make their decision. That's not good refereeing and it's not the proper use of the TMO either.

But, not only is it technology that scrutinises every match. That also happens before anyone's even trod on the pitch – in the days leading up to a match.

NO We are certainly more involved in the whole event days before the match now, which wasn't so true when you were refereeing. Coaches are allowed to meet with us the day before games during the international windows and talk to us about how we see various aspects of play, what our attitude to the breakdown is for example, or any questions we may have for them. I've always found this worthwhile but some referees find it a waste of time.

DB I'm not sure that has entirely improved the standard of refereeing though, I must say. It's still the case, as far as I can see, that some refs have a certain tendency to decide beforehand what kind of weaknesses one team or another, or one player or another, will show in the game they are about to referee. That means sometimes they will 'see' weaknesses not even there that day.

NO You can't do that. Players and coaches talk about playing what's in front of you. I think that's more than true for referees also. OK, it's easy to go into a game and think, such and such a player tends to do this, tends to infringe in this way or that way. But you can't go looking for that offence from that player. You're not being honest if you referee like that. It's far worse for a ref to give a dishonest performance than to give a bad performance. I always referee what's in front of me on match day, rather than go in with any preconceived ideas. A bit of preparation is good of course, but you need to have an open mind on the field. If you focus too much on certain players or one team, then the other team or opposition player may be getting away with doing exactly the same thing. That's not fair and consistent refereeing then.

DB There's one very important change we haven't mentioned yet – your pay is a lot better than anything I was ever used to! I had to fly out in economy to wherever I was going. I quite often had to cook my own breakfast in the hotel I'd been put in and buy my own shirts. That leads on to the whole thing about the role the ref has in today's game, I think. Right at the start of this book, that point is made clearly when the story of our crash is told. We were at the side of the M4, and a rugby referee was recognised by passers-by. That change in the profile and perception of referees is pretty much down to you, isn't it Nige?

NO I'm not the one to answer a question like that Bev, and you know it! Having said that, I'm more than aware of the whole discussion about how high a profile I should have in the public eye. I'm not oblivious to articles, such as the one by Austin Healey, asking if I'm now too much of a celebrity to referee some big games. I really think some context is called for here. I was involved in many forms of entertainment before my refereeing career took off. I took part in concerts and made TV appearances years ago. Certainly, years before people like Austin Healey knew who I was. I was used to performing before I was a ref. I don't count myself a celebrity at all. I'm well known, yes, of course. I would be lying if I said that I wasn't. But it's not something I took up the whistle to be. The fact that I came out as gay has also contributed to me being well known, without a doubt. I certainly don't referee to be famous. I referee because I

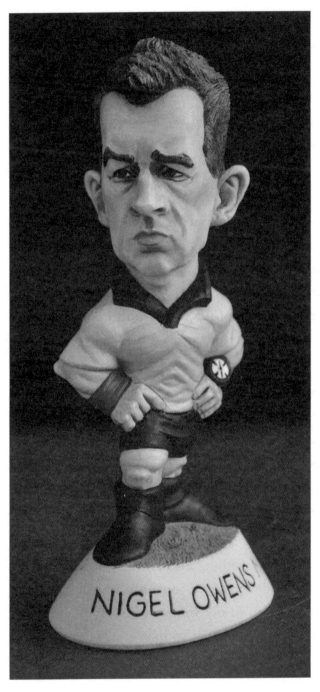

Not only are there Groggs for famous rugby players – Nigel has one too!

love the game. I love being a part of a global game, however small the part I play is.

DB So what you're saying is that, as you were already a TV performer, those opportunities increased when you then became a first-class referee.

NO Mmm, not quite, but obviously being a referee meant I was contributing to a variety of programmes about the game and things related to it. And the more I've progressed in the game, the more I've become well known, and the more well known I've become, the more the media opportunities arise, I guess. But a lot of the media stuff I do would have happened without the refereeing, I think.

DB I suppose, added to that, people need to consider that you are the kind of person who's also willing to talk openly about personal, emotional issues that have affected you. That's unusual in the rugby world, so people will turn to you more and more for that because there are not many others to turn to.

NO And that's not something I do for attention, or playing the media game, or whatever you want to call it. I know what I went through in my younger days and I've always wanted to be open about that so that others don't have to go through what I did. That has been more possible to do as my profile has increased. I'm not going to shy away from that.

DB I can't believe the profile you have now, I must say. I find it remarkable that a referee has the standing that you have. I remember the first time I saw it for myself. We were in France, in the rugby heartland of Toulouse. There's a bit of a walk from the dressing room to where the after-match function is held. It's a few hundred yards, but it's out in the open. I left the dressing room at the same time as you and got to the hospitality suite. You took a good 40 minutes to cover that short distance because of requests for selfies and autographs. I couldn't believe that – more than anything because we were in France! And then that was really driven home when a commentator on a WWE

It's been suggested that Nigel referees the Conor McGregor v Khabib Nurmagomedov rematch in UFC!

135

wrestling match said that he didn't think even Nigel Owens could solve a particular problem which arose in a wrestling match. Different country and different sport, yet you're mentioned!

NO I think this brings up a bigger point than just me. It says a lot about the role of the ref and it links in with what we talked about earlier, the use of mics and cameras during matches. It all revolves around increasing awareness about the ref so that people can understand the game itself better. Using mics is nothing to do with us wanting more attention. The thinking behind it was that if people could hear why a decision was made by us, then it would mean they understood the decision better and then understood the game better. It was a decision made to 'grow' the game. A major consequence of this is that it's brought the ref more into public perception. Some people say that I want my voice heard every time I referee, but that couldn't be further from the truth. I don't wear the ref's mic so that I can say my quips on the field. I wear it because I have to, and I don't make the quips because I am on the mic. I make them anyway. Always have. It's part of getting rugby to a wider audience and making those people understand what's going on better, especially if they are new to the game.

DB And some refs are going to take to that easier and more naturally than others. You, of course, were already used to cameras and microphones. I think a lot of fans misunderstand that, and think that the ref has taken on a greater significance, almost as if he is now an in-game coach and not the man there to apply the laws. That's not true at all. Nige, you probably don't do anything different to what I did reffing a game. But, because every word is heard and every move is seen now, some fans think that it's the refs that have got too big for their boots. That's a little short-sighted, to say the least.

But, regardless of the public profile, I think that your standing in the game throughout the world does say something definite about the way reffing is going in Wales at the moment.

NO What do you mean?

DB For me, it's quite a sad reflection that there's no one in Wales, certainly, to push you; there's no one to challenge you, to give you that competitive edge. There's no one, basically, who's up to your standard and can give you a run for your money. It's lucky, from your personal point of view, that you're self-motivated and not dependent on others to spur you on. But it says a lot about the lack of refs. When I reffed, there were four or five of us pushing each other, going for the top spots; five of us going for the three positions at the WRU, for example. That was good for Welsh rugby. It doesn't happen now. You just need to take your individual place on the world rankings.

NO You're right, I'm the one who motivates myself. That means I'm not the kind of ref who wants others to fail so that I can do better. I'm not the type to blow someone's candle out so that mine shines brighter. I don't work like that. But even though I get what you're saying about other refs in Wales today, I do think that there are more people wanting to be refs now than there were in your day. Being a ref is something that people aspire to, not like me and you who ended up as refs because we couldn't play any more, or because we just couldn't play! We have quite a few talented referees in Wales and I'm really excited for the future, watching them all come through. Hopefully they will take their place on the world refereeing panel.

DB That's true, fair point. It's encouraging that youngsters want to be refs now. That's new. But is it all good?

NO On the whole, of course it is. It means that people see that the referee is someone to be taken seriously in the game now, as much a part of any match as the players. But there are worrying signs, I must say. I can see that some want to be refs for the wrong reasons, because they see that refs can now have a high profile, can be well known. They choose to be refs in order to be well known within the game. That's totally the wrong way round. What I've already seen is that those who choose refereeing for the wrong reasons soon reach their plateau and many give up. Those who are in it because they love rugby and want to be referees – regardless

Nigel encouraging the next generation to become rugby referees

of what comes with it – they are the ones who will last and make an impression on the game.

DB Too true. Going back to the Austin Healey article you mentioned, they were comments made after a specific game, weren't they? Toulon were playing Munster and there was an incident at the start of the game when Toulon were apparently denied a penalty try. You obviously thought that there was no penalty try and therefore you needn't show

The match day team before Nigel referees France v South Africa in Paris in 2017. Nigel's great friend Wayne Barnes was assistant referee.

One of the toughest games Nigel's ever had to referee – France v Ireland in the 2018 Six Nations

anyone a yellow card. But, Toulon have a colourful owner in Mourad Boudjellal; he wasn't ever likely to let that kind of incident go without commenting on it. After the game he questioned whether it was right that a PRO14 ref should be in charge of a game between a PRO14 team and a French Top 14 team. But that wasn't your decision, was it Nige? You're given your games. You don't choose them, for goodness sake!

NO No, indeed. I think what that kind of story shows quite clearly, regardless of discussing its finer individual points, is that the role of the referee has changed completely now and it's an adjustment for all involved, the players, former players, the coaches, the broadcasters, the fans and the refs themselves. What people don't understand – and it's only us referees that really know this, I guess – is that there's no way a ref will favour one team over the other on the field. Absolutely no way. If I had to referee Wales for whatever reason, I would referee that match straight down the middle, no matter who they were playing. There's something in your DNA when you become a referee that makes sure you referee with integrity and fairness.

DB Enough about all that. Let's turn to something a little more pleasing as we bring our chat to an end. Let's both pick a game that we regard as our highlight. Mine is my highlight, as there won't be any more from me! But yours? We might need to call it your highlight so far.

NO I've got a few to choose from. It's going to be a job! The game at Croke Park I've already mentioned. Some of the European finals I've done. Ireland against New Zealand in Ireland. The World Cup final will always be the greatest moment or occasion for me, no doubt. But I suppose my choice as far as my best game is concerned would be South Africa against New Zealand in 2013. It's been called one of the best games there's ever been. So it's a natural for me to choose, I suppose.

DB It was an absolute cracker, that one in 2013! I'd have been very happy to be in charge of that one!

NO It was my first time refereeing at Ellis Park to start with, so that was special for me. But, more than that, the game itself was a deciding game in the Championship. If South Africa won with a bonus point and New Zealand didn't get a bonus point, then the 'Boks would be champions. If New Zealand won or got a bonus point, then they would be champions. That obviously helped the game a lot. Because, if the Springboks only needed to win, then they would have stuck the ball up their jumpers maybe, and played a close, tight game just to make sure they won. Like any other team would do. But, they really needed to score tries. New Zealand needed to score tries to get their bonus point, or to stay within seven points of South Africa of course. That meant that if South Africa were succeeding to score their tries, then New Zealand would have to make sure they were keeping up with them and staying within seven points. So an open game was always likely because of what was needed.

The end result says it all. The score was South Africa 27 New Zealand 38. There were nine tries in all, four to the Springboks and five to the All Blacks. The All Blacks clinched the fourth bonus point try they needed when their replacement fly-half touched down for a try – a certain Beauden Barrett! And Bryan Habana scored for the 'Boks before that as well. It was a masterful game of rugby.

I knew that on the field of play of course. Nine tries at that level speaks volumes. But it didn't really hit me properly until I walked off the pitch and into the ref's clubhouse – a particular South African feature! When I walked in, the other officials were there and they stood to applaud me. I then switched my mobile phone back on. The messages were flooding in, saying what a brilliant game it was and how it was brilliantly refereed. That's when it really hit me. That's when I really realised what I had been a part of. I had a phone call from one of the referees' selectors telling me that that was the best he'd ever seen me referee. That was just something else.

DB Back here in Wales the response was very similar. I remember an article in the *Western Mail* by Alun Wyn Jones. It wasn't about that game specifically, but he chose to refer to it in the paper, saying how great a game it was and how

Derek refereeing the Springboks versus Argentina, the late Joost van der Westhuizen's first cap

Nigel refereeing South Africa v New Zealand at Ellis Park in 2013 – a match that's been called one of the greatest games of rugby ever

well it had been refereed. I was nearly proud of you then, Nige!

NO Don't overdo it now, Bev! I was so lucky to have, not long after that, the New Zealand Ireland game I mentioned earlier. It was another cracker. I met with Joe Schmidt, the Irish coach, before the game and then I met Steve Hansen and his captain Richie McCaw. All this was part of the protocol I mentioned earlier when I said that refs now meet the coaches and captains the day before the game. As I left the meeting with McCaw and Hansen, McCaw turned to me and said, 'Let's hope tomorrow's game is as good as the last one.' My reply was, 'I don't think we'll see a game like that for a long time.' How wrong I was! That game in Dublin was also amazing. Ireland flew into the lead, 19–0 after 18 minutes, and the second half began with the All Blacks 22–7 down.

DB It was a real ding-dong second half wasn't it? New Zealand made it 22–17 with very little time left on the clock.

NO It was amazing! I penalised Ireland round about midfield and the All Blacks kept the ball for something like 20 phases and they ended up scoring a try. It was 22–22 with the conversion to come.

DB Up until that point Ireland were heading for what would have been a historic win for them against New Zealand. They had never beaten the All Blacks. It was Brian O'Driscoll's last game against the All Blacks and probably Paul O'Connell's as well. So there was no shortage of emotion and significance! That conversion, then, was critical. They might not win, with so little time left, but a draw was on for them if the conversion was missed. That's when things started to get a little challenging for you, Nige.

NO I remember it well! As a referee, you can't let yourself get involved in all the emotion and significance you mentioned just now. Now, looking back, I know that everyone wanted Ireland to win that day, unless you were a Kiwi of course. But I had to focus on what was happening there and then. As Aaron Cruden was about to take his kick, Tommy Bowe and Luke Fitzgerald started their run towards the kicker. But it was too early. I had noticed that and I remember thinking to myself, if Cruden misses this now, I'm going to have to ask him to take the kick again because the Irish boys charged far too early, and that's not allowed. Sure enough, he misses it. OK. Here goes, I think to myself. This fervent, enthusiastic, capacity Irish crowd are going to love this! It really was like a cauldron in there that day, with the Irish for most of the game sensing a famous victory. But I had to tell Cruden to take the kick again. He lines up for the conversion a second time. The kick sails through the posts with ease. It's 24–22 to the All Blacks.

DB You just so knew that that was going to happen, didn't you!

NO Absolutely.

DB What were you saying under your breath though, Nige?

NO Couldn't possibly comment again, Bev! After the final whistle, with the All Blacks winning on that last retaken conversion, I positioned myself as I always do near the touchline so that the players could come up to me if they wanted to. I'd never go to them – but make myself available if they wanted to come to me. It doesn't always happen, especially if a team has just suffered a difficult loss. I didn't expect a reaction from the Irish players but I did expect a difficult response from the Irish crowd. But I was surprised on both counts. As much as the Irish players were down on their knees with disappointment after a game they probably should have won, each one came up to me to shake my hand and say thank you. The crowd as well were very quiet and appreciative. That said a lot about Irish sportsmanship.

DB I bet you were walking on the ceiling Nige, and it was very difficult to get you back down!

NO Maybe I was! Anyway, what about the game you remember best?

DB Well, unlike you, I will actually only choose one! It's a simple choice for me. It's the opening game of the 1995 World Cup. It was held in South Africa and it was the first time they had been allowed to participate in the World Cup following years of exclusion because of apartheid-related issues. So, in that sense alone, it was a historic occasion, not just in terms of rugby but on a wider political and historical front too.

NO Sounds to me that that kind of situation added a great deal to the occasion and made it more significant than it would otherwise have been.

DB That's the point. I was extremely nervous before that game, more than for most games I'd ever refereed in my career. The opening ceremony was one that was full of colour. You can imagine the various tribes that they have in South Africa, and many were represented at the ceremony. So there was colour, music and atmosphere I hadn't experienced before. It was the Rainbow Nation on display! Then, into this arena steps Nelson Mandela. Waw! What a presence. He famously wore a South African rugby shirt for that event, which immediately struck the right chord on all fronts. He was identifying with his nation and the occasion as a recently freed black man and president of his country. It was very powerful.

NO I can't imagine what that was like. But, without wishing to take anything away from that, and I really wouldn't, you had to show your total refereeing impartiality even in the middle of such an occasion, didn't you?

DB I did indeed. Before the honour of meeting Mandela and the South African and Australian teams on the pitch, I had to do my usual dressing room inspections. I went into the South African dressing room and saw a room full of what looked like American Football players. They were padded to the hilt on every possible part of the body. So I spoke to them collectively and asked if this was their kit for the warm-up. They said no; this was how they were going to play the game. I said that, if that was the case, then I wouldn't allow them on the pitch and Australia would go through by default. Within two minutes an alternative kit was found, having been told that there wasn't one available, and they took to the field wearing what was actually allowed.

NO That's what you call one of those tough decisions! Just goes to show, doesn't it, that whatever the occasion you just have to referee the match.

DB You really do. But that's not what stays in my memory

Derek has had the privilege of meeting many inspiring people, including Nelson Mandela and Sir Gary Sobers

all these years later. The lasting memory is Mandela in his rugby shirt on that pitch. I am so appreciative that rugby has been my life for so long, and it has given me so much. But meeting Mandela reminded me that rugby isn't actually life itself.

And finally…

NO I've been very good so far and have not mentioned a certain incident between us that has gone down in rugby folklore. But, deep into injury time, I'm going to sneak it in!

DB I thought it was too good to be true that you hadn't mentioned the Blues Ospreys game four years ago!

NO Rhys Webb had just managed to get over the line and ground the ball under a pile of bodies for a try, giving the Ospreys their bonus point. But I wanted to double-check if it was a try or not. So, I called up to you. The conversation is on YouTube and has had nearly 120,000 viewings. It went like this:

'Derek.'

'Hello Nige.'

'Any reason why I can't award the try?'

'Any reason why you can't award the try?'

As TMO, Derek worked with Nigel for the last time at a match in Toulouse. Here they are with Rhys Davies and Gwyn Morris.

'Yes. He was on his back on the line, so no double movement or holding on.'

Then, after studying the move in detail, looking at the various camera angles, you came back with your deliberation:

'Nige!'

'Hello Derek.'

'There's no reason I can't give you that you cannot award a try.'

'There's no reason why I can't award the try. (Pause) So I can award the try?'

'That is it.'

DB Watching that back after, the little smile playing on your face as you hear my answer and then try to understand what I said is really funny. I had a bad dose of the double negatives that day, to be sure! But we certainly had a good laugh about it, as has everyone else!

Also from Y Lolfa:

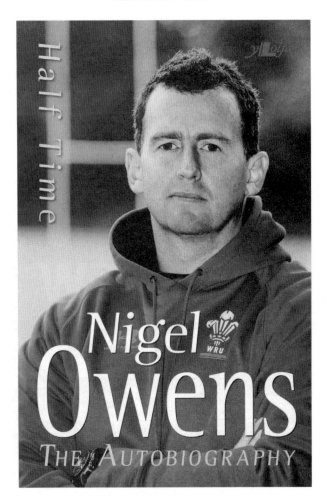

£9.95

y Lolfa

MATTHEW REES

REASONS 2 SMILE

MY BATTLES ON AND OFF THE RUGBY FIELD

FOREWORD BY WARREN GATLAND

£9.99

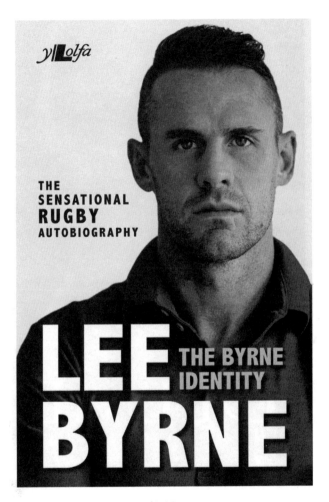

y Lolfa

**THE
SENSATIONAL
RUGBY
AUTOBIOGRAPHY**

LEE
THE BYRNE
IDENTITY
BYRNE

£9.99

DELME
THE AUTOBIOGRAPHY

with Alun Gibbard

£9.95

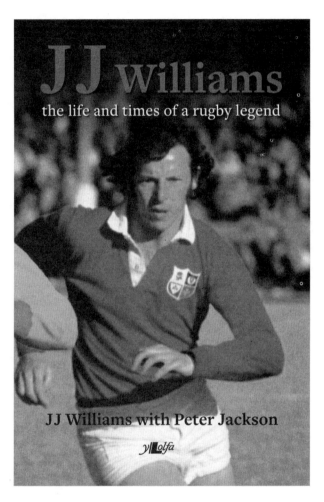

JJ Williams

the life and times of a rugby legend

JJ Williams with Peter Jackson

y Lolfa

£14.99
(hardback)

Derek and Nigel is just one of a whole range
of publications from Y Lolfa. For a full list of
books currently in print, send now for your
free copy of our new full-colour catalogue.
Or simply surf into our website

www.ylolfa.com

for secure on-line ordering.

TALYBONT CEREDIGION CYMRU SY24 5HE
e-mail ylolfa@ylolfa.com
website www.ylolfa.com
phone (01970) 832 304
fax 832 782